SEEING THE
BIOPHARMA FUTURE

Bradon,

Thanks so much for your support
& making this book possible. I hope
all is well with you in Nashville in
the midst of COVID-19. I heard that
state-wide, TN has free testing.

SEEING THE BIOPHARMA FUTURE

ABRA SITLER

NEW DEGREE PRESS

SEEING THE BIOPHARMA FUTURE

ISBN   978-1-64137-426-2 *Paperback*
         978-1-64137-427-9 *Kindle Ebook*
         978-1-64137-428-6 *Ebook*

CONTENTS

—

EARLY PRAISE
FOR SEEING THE
BIOPHARMA FUTURE

———

"In Seeing the Biopharma Future, Abra Sitler makes one of the most compelling arguments for investing in precision medicine technology to date. Given her experience and firsthand knowledge as both a consumer and a working professional inside the American Healthcare system, she is uniquely qualified to explore some of the system's biggest challenges and areas for improvement. This book is a must-read for anyone looking for hope in the healthcare system and a better understanding of what's to come for the future of precision medicine."

—RYAN PORTER, BUSINESS CONSULTANT.

ACKNOWLEDGMENTS

———

Writing this book has been a unique opportunity to learn more about genetics, healthcare, biotechnology, and pharmaceuticals. It also led me to have many fascinating conversations and interviews, to develop new ideas, and to grow personally and professionally. It gave me a career path during my MBA and allowed me to explore my own connection to the enormous healthcare industry. Through the process of writing this, I articulated my own personal and professional vision for the future.

I would like to thank my family for always supporting me and for believing that I can accomplish whatever I set my mind on. I often overextend myself, but my family has always been there to help. I would like to thank friends who have encouraged me throughout this journey and have helped share my message with others. I want to give a special acknowledgment to my sisters, Ariel and Anna Sitler, for helping me become who I am today. Writing this book, starting a new career, and finishing my MBA could not be done if I didn't have you making me a better person every day.

Special thanks must go to Professor Eric Koester, who first inspired me to write a book while at Georgetown. "There's never a good time to write a book," he said when I expressed concern about having enough time. He was right. I want to thank Brian Bies for continuing to work with me in the toughest moments. Eric and Brian have stayed on me and have shown some of the best leadership and motivational skills I have seen. They got me over the fear of putting myself out there to write this. They gave me an extra nudge whenever needed and broke down what felt like an impossible task into a manageable and inspiring journey that has been transformative.

I want to thank Ryan Porter for his patience and dedication, and for teaching me how to be a better editor, marketer, and writer. I also want to thank my editors Michelle Feliche, Cynthia Tucker, Leila Summers, and Amanda Brown for helping make this a better book.

I want to thank those who took the time to interview with me, sharing their perspectives and insights on the past, present, and future of biopharmaceuticals. Lastly, I want to acknowledge anyone who has supported me throughout this process, who has pre-ordered this book, and anyone buying it when it releases. This book is a first step for me into a brighter future in this industry. Thanks to Kenna and Walt Levendosky, Ariel Sitler, Lara Sitler, George Sitler, Anna Sitler, Sarah ElHoss, Marki Dittman, Kevin Schlosser, Zac Cromie, Nora Browning, Thilanka Munasinghe, Neda Hosseini, Kristen E. Ross, Cory Alan Camechis Smith, Caitlin Berard, Alaa Kamnaksh, Betsy Trovato, Blake Carpenter, Trevor Earnshaw, Beatrice Gendre, Clark Webber, Karin Johnson, Robert

Boorstin, Andrew Cavazos, Claire Garner, Michael Montafi, Zihao Liu, Angela Corbin, Michael kim, Christina Levendosky, Braden Clark, Benjamin Pitzer, Marki Allegar, Amy Baldwin, Charlotte Clark, Tess Meinert, James Teachen, Cat McConnell, Robert Sturm, Nate Askins, Joel Manner, Adam Komisaruk, Chong Hwan Kim, Hannah Nickerson, Jory Callahan, Anna Khandros, Spencer Leo, Manesha Sampath, Guillermo Olortegui, William Staniland, Alisa Bellamy, Snowdave8, Rachel Cosgray, Tia Caldwell, Stanley He, Olivia McConnell, Scott Johnson, Alanna Markle, Julian Haas, Brett Cotton, Janice Cabrera-Frias, Sadiyyah Owens, Blair Stanford, Diane Khatib, Ahlia Sekkarie, Rebecca Levy, Nikhil Sud, Eric Koester, Jennie Reams, Rob Burke, Tyler Zanini, Maude Champagne, David Kodak, Ronald Peppin, Shannon Goudy, and Robert Preziosi.

"Life is creative in the strongest possible sense."

—*ANTOINE DANCHIN*[1]

---

1   Danchin, Antoine. *The Delphic Boat*. Harvard University Press. 2002.

PART 1:

WHY I WROTE THIS BOOK AND CHALLENGES IN THE U.S. HEALTHCARE SYSTEM

INTRODUCTION

"We are at a turning point—never again will we understand life, or organize the way we think about it, in quite the same way."
—ANTOINE DANCHIN[2]

When I was fourteen years old, I started to lose my vision. I was no longer able to see the letters on the chalkboard of my high school geometry class and couldn't read subtitles on a foreign film or menu options at a restaurant. I couldn't recognize my friends and family until they were ten feet away. Doctors didn't know or understand why.

I was prescribed glasses that couldn't correct the problem. I visited doctors around the country, and, for several years, they couldn't explain how a young, healthy teenager could go from having perfect vision to having the vision of an elderly adult. Finally, I was diagnosed with a rare genetic condition called Stargardt's disease. The doctors said, "Monitor your eyes and check in, but there's nothing we can do."

---

2   Danchin, Antoine. *The Delphic Boat*. Harvard University Press. 2002.

Their answer wasn't helpful, and I wondered if I could ever hope for more. Years later, I visited a doctor who talked to me about the future of gene therapy and some of the progress being made. "I believe in fifteen years there will be something we can do for you," she said. "Keep reading and following new developments. I am sure we will have something in your lifetime." She gave me hope to believe—and to see—that there was more promise to advances in genetics than some doctors believed or even realized.

From this experience, I saw that the current pace of research and development was outpacing our ability, including physicians,' to keep up. My genetic condition is invisible to most people; so, too, is much of the progress we are making in biotechnology. We are facing a new frontier that will significantly change our current healthcare system. The system we have today wasn't designed to treat or finance patients in a personalized way, yet the era of precision medicine— brought about by advances in technology, computer science, and genetics—is here. With the right investments, these advances have the potential to dramatically improve our current model.

As of 2019, the United States has the world's most expensive healthcare system.[3] Furthermore, the cost of healthcare, drug research and development, and health insurance are all rising—driving us toward an even less sustainable future. Despite being one of the wealthiest countries in the world with the most expensive care, the World Health

---

3   Anon 2020. *Who.Int.*

Organization ranks the quality of the U.S. healthcare system as thirty-seventh globally.[4]

The National Institute of Health reports that of the 7,000 rare diseases that we know of today, the number of U.S. Food and Drug Administration-approved treatments for rare disease is less than 5 percent.[5] It also estimates that as much as 10 percent of the U.S. population has a rare disease. Despite this relatively high percentage and the high cost of care, the U.S. healthcare system isn't working for most patients with rare diseases or for the general public.

The most concerning fact about our current healthcare system is that positive health outcomes for patients are on the decline. A report released by the Centers for Disease Control in 2017 concluded that life expectancy in the U.S. has been declining for the last three years.[6] Now countries with smaller economies, lower income, less expensive care, and limited access to treatment and technology have longer life spans and more effective health care systems.

Recent advances in biotechnology have the potential to address some key problems in today's U.S. healthcare system. Today, we have more technology and information than ever before to treat disease. What we have to do as consumers is to learn about, invest in, and advocate for them and their potential. Our healthcare system needs attention and repair—we need a moonshot, or a "health shot."

---

4   Ibid.
5   Anon2020. *Report.Nih.gov.*
6   Devitt, Michael. 2020. "CDC Data Show U.S. Life Expectancy Continues To Decline." *Aafp.org.*

The consensus among many of my colleagues is that subjects like biotechnology and healthcare are too difficult to understand. My intent in writing this book is to make what may seem like inaccessible information, ideas, and treatments in precision medicine more accessible to you. My hope is to improve your understanding of how the biopharma industry works, why our health care system has some of the challenges it does today, and how collective and informed investments in precision medicine can improve it. Some of these recent advances in genetics are issues we can all understand that have the potential to impact many aspects of our day-to-day health as individuals and as a global society.

For the last fifteen years, I've followed the development of clinical trials, experimental drugs, and developments in the biotech industry to better understand how they will impact me as a patient and, more broadly, society and the healthcare system as a whole. Guided by the words of the doctor who told me to not lose hope, and to continue seeking treatment, I've studied how these developments can be expanded to patients with a host of other illnesses and may even be used as preventative treatments. Through this journey to understand my own condition and not lose sight of advances being made, I've gathered perspectives from some of the scientific community's best thinkers, geneticists, researchers, investment bankers, doctors, insurers, drug developers, and regulators to develop a holistic understanding of our current system. It led me down the path of compiling these ideas and perspectives into this book, and to my next professional role working in Business Insights and Analytics at Bristol Myers Squibb in Princeton, New Jersey.

This book includes perspectives from Victor Li and Antoine Danchin, geneticists who worked on the Human Genome Project; Jennifer Doudna, a co-discoverer of CRISPR-Cas9 gene-editing technology; and physicians at the Wills Eye Institute in Philadelphia and Johns Hopkins in Baltimore. I've also included international perspectives from French scientist and diplomat Francois Gendre, and from physicians in Lyon, France, which, according to the WHO, has the highest quality healthcare system in the world.[7] The discoveries and progress being made are truly global and are impacting healthcare systems around the world beyond the U.S.

My goal in writing this book is to share these perspectives and inform you about exciting advances being made that have the potential to treat conditions previously untreatable, improve the longevity and quality of our lives, and improve our healthcare system. George Church, a Harvard professor and geneticist, said, "We now understand enough about genetics to reverse some of the effects of aging in eight different ways through adding genes, currently in mice—one day it could be in humans."

This book explores three major breakthroughs in biotech in the last twenty years that bring us to this life sciences revolution and new scientific frontiers. These breakthroughs are not only revolutionizing the way we develop and understand drugs but are also changing the way we deliver patient care. The first major breakthrough this book explores is our recent ability to efficiently and cost effectively sequence a patient's genome, or the human blueprint. The human genome was

---

7   Anon 2020. *Who.Int.*

first sequenced in 2003, over a span of fifteen years, and cost over three billion dollars.[8] Today, we can sequence a patient's complete genome in a matter of hours for $1,000. Soon, it will be $100 and take less time.[9] Our genome is the blueprint that may enable us to better study and understand our health and how we can improve it. Little is understood about all our genome does today, but it has only been within our lifetimes that we could even sequence it.

The second breakthrough is the discovery of CRISPR Cas9 gene-editing technology. We now, for the first time, have a tool to precisely and efficiently edit genes. What this means is that we have the ability to edit the human genome; we can edit a gene mutation causing a hereditary disease and potentially treat the patient. This technology implies that we can also change someone's eye color, give them immunity to a disease, or make them less prone to diabetes or heart disease. This is an incredibly powerful tool that fundamentally reshapes how we think about treating disease. It is a technology that drug makers and governments around the world are investing in. This newfound capability not only presents us with powerful tools through which to remedy many diseases, but also poses ethical questions about the societal implications of gene editing and how this technology should be responsibly used. These technologies pose fundamental questions about what it means to be human and what we will do with them.

---

8   "International Consortium Completes Human Genome Project." 2020. Genome.gov.

9   "The Cost Of Sequencing A Human Genome." 2020. Genome.gov.

Lastly, this book addresses advances in computer science, artificial intelligence, and analytic tools that enable us to more rapidly identify patterns in the genome, analyze sequences, and understand how genes work—collectively and individually. We are entering a new frontier where computer science and biology are no longer two separate disciplines. Instead, they are being combined into a new field: computational biology. These breakthroughs are changing how we develop and prescribe drugs, how we evaluate and diagnose patients, and how we decide to treat them. Today, we have more precise, effective drugs than ever, and the advances and discoveries we make are happening faster than ever before.

This book is written to give hope and inspiration to the scientifically curious, to people who have been told there is no solution for their disease. It's for those who believe we need to invest in a more effective, innovative health care system that improves and lengthens our lives. We now have the tools to sequence every person's genome, and to treat patients in a personalized way that fits their genetic makeup for more effective outcomes. The implications of these three discoveries are already showing results today. Our challenge is to understand the relationships between genetic makeup and external factors, such as diet or lifestyle. It is also to understand the relationship between our genetic makeup and how our bodies function—on a microscopic and macroscopic level—and apply this to patient care.

In the U.S. healthcare system, it's easy to be overlooked. Our current system is not set up to finance and manage the amount of data and treatments we now have available to deliver more precise care. Doctors increasingly rely on patients to advocate for their own treatment and health outcomes. The pace at which new drugs, therapies, and treatments are being developed has outpaced many physicians' ability to keep up. Genetics is still a new field, as is computational biology. Many practicing physicians today didn't study these fields in their medical education. Simply put, many of these breakthroughs and discoveries hadn't happened and didn't exist.

Like choosing a menu option at a restaurant, our current health care model requires consumers to make choices not only based on price but on effectiveness. To take control of our own health, we have to educate ourselves about existing research, emerging treatment options, and potential future options. We'll have to understand the importance of our unique blueprint to our health—how much is based in genetics and how much in the environment. "The knowledge of the whole genome not only makes life easier to understand but also places life totally beyond the reach of commonsense prediction," wrote Antoine Danchin.[10] These recent advances are in the early stages of development but can be accelerated toward better health if we choose to see, engage with, and invest in our biopharma future.

10   Danchin, Antoine. *The Delphic Boat.* Harvard University Press. 2002.

CHAPTER 1:

SEEING THE PRECISION MEDICINE POTENTIAL

"This life of yours which you are living is not merely a piece of the entire existence, but is in a certain sense the whole; only this whole is not so constituted that it can be surveyed in one single glance."

—ERWIN SCHRÖDINGER

SEEING THE WORLD THROUGH STARGARDT'S DISEASE

Imagine looking at a projector with thousands of holes punched through the paper. You can make out some of the images, but there are gaps in what you see. Through those holes flash neon lights that swirl around letters and shapes, many of which you cannot see. You know the images are steady, but they shake in and out of focus. You know that the way you are seeing the world isn't the way most see it. You guess some of the words and letters you are missing. You fill in the holes with your mind—you imagine what you don't see.

When someone is walking toward me, I recognize them by the way they move rather than their face, or I listen to the sound of their voice and steps. I've learned to look around what I can't see and relate my senses to one another to infer what is otherwise invisible. This is how I see the world— relating sensations through context, clues, and with some imagination.

Because it happened gradually, I didn't know I was losing my vision. I didn't have a reference for others seeing the world differently until they saw me reading or mentioned they'd said hello and I didn't seem to recognize them. People often think, and I thought, that I wasn't paying attention to what they saw.

I remember sitting in geometry class in high school. I couldn't make out the shapes, angles, measurements, and long-winded equations my teacher outlined on the chalk-board. So, I listened. Through listening and guesswork, I followed as much as I could. I assumed everyone thought geometry was hard and that no one else could see what the teacher was writing either.

Eventually, I was called in for a school vision test, where I was asked to look through a pair of binoculars on a machine. "Look inside," they said.
"What am I supposed to be looking at?" I asked. "There isn't anything here."
They thought I was joking.
"The letters," they said impatiently, "read them."
I looked back, confused. "There aren't any letters."
I had completely failed the vision exam.

After being diagnosed with Stargardt's disease at the age of fourteen and being told I would keep losing my vision throughout my life, I began looking at the world differently. At first, and for a long time, I tried to hide it. Mostly, it worked. As sight is only one of our senses, it would be blind to measure an individual's ability with a vision chart of still letters. While I've lost much of my vision, I've also opened up to seeing a whole new world.

Today, I notice the advances we are making in biotechnology and the new software tools we develop to make adaptation possible to almost any task. I pay attention to how we are making discoveries and advances that have the potential to treat diseases such as my own—and multitudes of others—in the collective movement we are terming "precision medicine."

THE MODERN PRECISION MEDICINE ERA AND WHAT WE MEAN BY IT

We are entering a new phase in medical advances and technology. According to the National Institute of Health and the Precision Medicine Initiative, precision medicine is "an emerging approach for disease treatment and prevention that takes into account individual variability in genes, environment, and lifestyle for each person."[11] Approaching patient treatment through an individual lens allows doctors and researchers to predict more accurately which treatment and prevention strategies for a particular disease will work in which groups of people. This contrasts with a one-size-fits-all

---

11   Reference, Genetics. 2020. "What Is Precision Medicine?" Genetics Home Reference.

approach in which disease prevention and treatment strategies have been developed for the "average person," which had less consideration for differences between individuals. A few key discoveries are and will continue to be integral to this personalized patient approach.

Firstly, understanding the genome and its sequencing has enabled us to begin understanding some causes of and links to diseases, such as cancer and rare gene mutations. Rather than having a vague idea, guessing, or giving a general diagnosis of a patient's illness, we can instead sequence their genome to understand underpinning causes. We can more closely monitor disease progression and use the genome to predict what other illnesses or diseases a patient may be susceptible to. An example of two genes we understand and can link to cancer are the BRCA1 and BRCA2 genes that produce tumor-suppressing proteins.[12] For example, mutations of these two genes in patients are associated with a higher chance of developing breast cancer or ovarian cancer in women, and additional risk for developing several other types of cancer. By sequencing the patient's genome, we can more closely monitor for cancer and begin detection and treatment earlier. This approach ultimately increases survival probability and offers more positive, healthier outcomes.[13] This is an example of a practice that is becoming more widespread in clinics and hospitals around the world.[14]

---

12   "BRCA Mutations: Cancer Risk And Genetic Testing Fact Sheet." 2020. National Cancer Institute.

13   Ibid.

14   NIH Research Portfolio Online Reporting Tools (Report) "NIH Research Portfolio Online Reporting Tools (Report)." 2020. Report. Nih.gov.

THE THREE ERAS OF BIOTECHNOLOGY

The term "biotechnology" was first used by Karl Ereky, a Hungarian engineer, in 1919.[15] One definition of biotechnology is "...the application of the principles of engineering and biological science to create new products from raw materials of biological origin, like vaccines or food."[16] Significant discoveries and advances in biology, engineering, and technology over the last fifty years have prompted an increased use of this term. Broadly, we can break biotechnology into three eras—ancient, classical, and modern. New discoveries are building on previous ones and are creating new possibilities and synergies between ideas, technology, engineering principles, and biological principles.

From fiction, myth, and reality, biotechnology can be simply understood from the novel *Frankenstein* by Mary Shelley. In this story, Frankenstein creates life from human remains, which then became a monster. While the engineering principles in this story are not those used in today's genetic engineering, the idea and end product of creating or engineering life is now possible.[17]

15 Verma, AshishSwarup, Shruti Rastogi, Shishir Agrahari, and Anchal Singh. 2011. "Biotechnology In The Realm Of History." Journal Of Pharmacy And Bioallied Sciences 3 (3): 321. doi:10.4103/0975-7406.84430.

16 Ibid.

17 Verma, AshishSwarup, Shruti Rastogi, Shishir Agrahari, and Anchal Singh. 2011. "Biotechnology In The Realm Of History." Journal Of Pharmacy And Bioallied Sciences 3 (3): 321. doi:10.4103/0975-7406.84430.

HISTORY OF THE DEVELOPMENT OF BIOTECHNOLOGY: ANCIENT, CLASSIC, AND MODERN

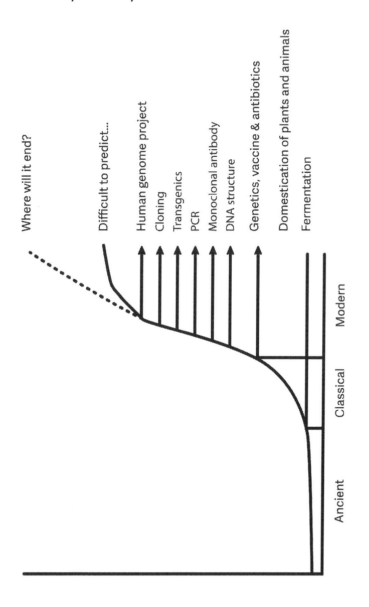

ANCIENT BIOTECHNOLOGY

This period runs until 1800 and marks agricultural development and the domestication of crops and wild animals to breed for certain characteristics to control food production. In this era, we discovered the use of microbes to develop cheese, yeast to make bread, and fermentation to make vinegar and alcohol. In this era, we learned how to preserve and sterilize food and water, all for the betterment of human life. [18]

CLASSICAL BIOTECHNOLOGY

This period is generally marked from the 1800s to the mid-twentieth century. During this time, Gregor Mendel conducted his pea plant experiment and described his findings—known as the laws of inheritance—in which he concluded invisible internal units of information account for observable traits, and that these "factors" are passed from one generation to the next.[19] Charles Darwin visited the Galapagos Islands and proposed his theory of evolution. The nucleus in Eukaryota cells was discovered by Robert Brown in 1868, the same year Friedrich Miescher reported nuclein, a compound that consisted of nucleic acid extracted from white blood cells. These two discoveries ultimately became the basis for molecular biology. The theory of the gene was proposed in 1926 from T.H. Morgan's fruit fly experiments. Alexander Fleming developed penicillin,

---

18 Ibid.
19 Verma, AshishSwarup, Shruti Rastogi, Shishir Agrahari, and Anchal Singh. 2011. "Biotechnology In The Realm Of History." Journal Of Pharmacy And Bioallied Sciences 3 (3): 321. doi:10.4103/0975-7406.84430.

the basis for administration-approved antibiotics, and we developed the smallpox vaccine.[20]

MODERN BIOTECHNOLOGY

In this period, the DNA double helix structure is discovered, laying the foundation for many discoveries in the present day. This will be explored in detail in Chapter 5.

THE TRANSITION FROM PHARMACEUTICAL TO BIOPHARMACEUTICAL

In Modern Biotechnology, the biopharmaceuticals market has developed much faster than the market for all drugs and is believed to have great potential for further dynamic growth. Biopharmaceuticals are medical drugs produced using biotechnology—that is, therapeutic products created through genetic manipulation of living cells or organisms.[21] The primary distinction between biopharma and pharma products is in the manufacturing process, discussed in chapter 14. Biopharmaceuticals are manufactured in living organisms such as bacteria, yeast, and mammalian cells. Pharmaceuticals are manufactured through a series of chemical synthesis. So think of prescribing patients cellular-based therapies rather than pills—this is what we mean by "biopharmaceutical."

---

20 Ibid.
21 David O'Riordan Engineers Ireland. 2013. "Transitioning From Traditional Pharmaceuticals To Biopharma – Engineers Journal." Engineers Journal.

In the biopharmaceutical era, we are more able to tailor treatments to patients than ever before. We use data from genetic sequences, compare this to other sequences to identify diseases and gene mutations, issue stem cell and gene therapies, and even edit genomes to create custom treatments. This is the power of precision medicine.

My beginning with Stargardt's disease was only fifteen years ago. Each of my doctors had different opinions about my vision and what my future could look like as a patient. While some physicians told me there was nothing that could be done, today there are gene and stem therapies in clinical trials to regenerate and preserve vision for Stargardt's patients. The experience of undergoing the same evaluations but being given different opinions fascinated me. Each physician conducted nearly the same evaluations but then engaged in a certain amount of guesswork. For several years, I encountered many explanations for the source of my problem. What was most confusing to my physicians was that my vision was worsening despite being given new glasses each year and being otherwise healthy.

Finally, I visited a pediatric ophthalmologist at the West Virginia University Eye Institute. Dr. Schwartz, the diagnosing physician, ran one last test that injected dye into my arm, then photographing the appearance of the dye in my eyes moments later. Pigments of yellow dye flecked near the retina meant I probably had Stargardt's disease. However, this could only be definitively confirmed with a genetic test. At the time, a genetic test cost over $50,000 and wasn't covered by insurance. She recommended I wait. "The technology will improve," she said. Years later, when the cost was reduced to

$1,000 and could be covered by insurance, I had a genetic test done at Johns Hopkins. This was a truly precise mechanism to formally diagnose the disease. The results were positive.

GENETICS UNDERPINS STARGARDT'S DISEASE

According to the National Eye Institute, Stargardt's disease is a genetically inherited form of juvenile macular degeneration.[22] What this means is that a patient begins losing their central vision at a young age in the macula—the part of the eye near the retina's center—and is responsible for our high-resolution color vision that is possible in good lighting. Our central vision is what we use to discern detail, for example reading and recognizing faces. Stargardt's causes gradual central vision loss, which becomes noticeable during puberty in most patients. The cause of Stargardt's disease is a genetic mutation in the ABCA4 gene, which is the sequence for a protein that removes Vitamin A byproducts from photoreceptor cells.[23] This gene is only expressed in the retina. So, its mutation causes Stargardt's disease and affects the retina and central vision but doesn't affect other parts of the body, as it isn't a gene expressed elsewhere.

We usually think of Vitamin A as being good for our eye health, which is why we eat an abundance of carrots, sweet potatoes, and pumpkins.[24] For a Stargardt's patient, too much Vitamin A only worsens our vision and damages our

---

22 "Stargardt's Disease | National Eye Institute." 2020. Nei.Nih.gov.
23 Ibid.
24 "Vitamin A." 2020. Mayo Clinic.

photoreceptor cells.[25] Photoreceptor cells absorb photons, or light, and send a signal to the brain. Photoreceptor cells are also known as rods and cones. These work together to send an electric signal to the brain, which enables us to see. Rods are in the outer part of the retina and enable us to sense light and darkness; cones are in the macula and help us discern colors and finer details.[26]

So, what happens to photoreceptor cells in a Stargardt's patient? When we ingest foods rich in Vitamin A, the photoreceptor cells with the mutation of the ABCA4 gene don't produce the protein that remove byproducts. The result is an accumulation of lipofuscin, which is a fatty substance that forms yellowish specks. This is why the dye test is used to detect Stargardt's—the yellow pigmentation enhances the visibility of accumulated lipofuscin.[27]

This buildup causes damage and eventually death to photoreceptor cells, particularly in the macula. The result is fewer cells are able to absorb light and send signals to the brain, leading to distortion in the central vision. This boils down to a decreased ability to read, to recognize faces, to discern detail, and to focus. While my own peripheral vision—or the vision we use to detect movement and to "see out of the corner of our eyes"—is mostly unaffected, it is the central vision and macula that are affected by the disease.

---

25 "Stargardt's Disease Vitamin A Contraindication – Natural Eye Care Blog: News & Research On Vision." 2012. Natural Eye Care Blog: News & Research On Vision.

26 "An Eye To A Cure." 2011. NIH Intramural Research Program.

27 "Lipofuscin: Medlineplus Medical Encyclopedia." 2020. Medlineplus. gov.

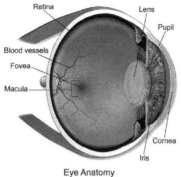

Eye Anatomy

With a gradual decrease in my visual acuity, I rely a lot on my mind, memory, context, clues, and other senses to fill in details I can't see. This means I can still drive, ride my bike, and run. I can detect motion and things out of the corner of my eye. However, it means something else for reading and working on the computer. This is an example of the distortion I see in my central vision.[28]

---

28 "Stargardt's Disease | National Eye Institute." 2020. Nei.Nih.gov.

I've found ways to adapt to my decreasing eyesight, but my vision isn't getting better. With time, it may grow. Here's an example of a Stargardt's patient and their affected eye health. [29]

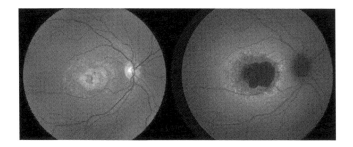

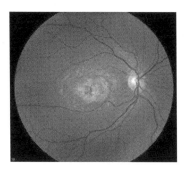

The images above are taken from a Stargardt's patient and show a central macular scar with some pigmentary changes and surrounding paramacular flecks. They illustrate the damage done to the macula over time.[30]

29 "Stargardt's Disease | National Eye Institute." 2020. Nei.Nih.gov.
30 "Stargardt's Disease | National Eye Institute." 2020. Nei.Nih.gov.

And, finally, below is an example of a healthy macula in a patient *without* Stargardt's disease. There is no inflammation visible in the macula; the tissue is healthy and normal.

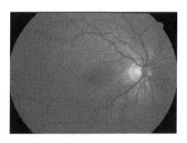

STARGARDT'S GENE MUTATION AND INHERITED DISEASE

Stargardt's disease is genetically inherited and can be found on a double recessive gene. A double recessive gene means it was inherited from both parents, even if the gene wasn't expressed in one or the other. This dynamic is represented in the blue square of Gregor Mendel's Dominant and Recessive gene chart.

After writing about the laws of inheritance, Gregor Mendel was credited as the founder of modern genetics. He is known in particular for coining the terms "dominant" and "recessive" in relation to traits through his pea pod experiment. In these experiments, he noted certain physical characteristics of the pea pods and labeled them. Mendel would grow a set of peas and note some of their traits, such as size or color. He would then cross-breed different pea plants with one another and make observations about the offspring. He would note which pea plants were yellow, which were green, which were small or large, and note if these traits were "passed down" to the offspring. Mendel repeated the process, each time, noting the physical traits of the pea plant parents and offspring. Dominant genes, he noted, had a higher probability of being expressed in offspring than recessive genes. For a double recessive gene to be inherited, Mendel realized the recessive gene, for example, yellow peas, had to be present in both parents.[31]

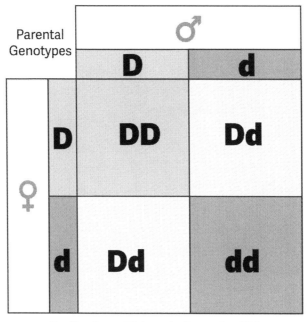

D = Dominant Allele   d = Recessive Allele

---

31 "Mendel's Laws: Law Of Independent Assortment, Segregation, Dominance, Inheritance." 2017. Science ABC.

Genes are bundled together in chromosomes. A copy of each chromosome is passed on from each parent at conception, when a sperm fertilizes an egg. The X and Y chromosomes are the sex chromosomes. So a person with XX sex chromosomes is biologically female, while XY is male.

As Stargardt's is an autosomal recessive trait, it takes two copies of the mutated gene—one from each parent—for the gene to be present and expressed. While neither of my parents has the disease, it would be present as Aa and Aa for both of them, meaning they both carried the Stargardt's gene mutation without expression. I inherited the aa, or autosomal, recessive form. One "little a" came from my mother, and one "little a" from my father, causing it to be present and expressed in my genetic makeup.

Using the chart, when two parents carry but don't express the gene, we have these probabilities that they will pass it down to their offspring:

- 25 percent chance of having the gene (aa).
- 25 percent chance of not having the gene (AA).
- 50 percent chance of having the gene, but not expressing (Aa).

WHAT THE BIOPHARMA FUTURE HOLDS FOR PATIENTS

We live in the modern era of biotechnology, when the human genome has been mapped and new, more precise targeted treatments like gene therapies are emerging. Thankfully, Dr. Schwartz encouraged me to continue seeing a geneticist and ophthalmologist throughout my life.

I now see a physician at Johns Hopkins who conducts stem cell and gene therapy research, which weren't legally approved as recently as the George W. Bush administration.[32] As of only a few years ago, there were very few people studying Stargardt's, hence my misdiagnosis. I believe this exponential progress, in conjunction with Moore's Law, will continue, particularly as more people become aware of advances and begin to see their potential to improve their own health outcomes.[33] We've come a long way: from developing vinegar to preserve food to now developing gene therapies to treat people with genetic diseases. We can only imagine what the future may hold for the betterment of human life if we choose to envision and invest in our biopharma future. The first step may be to have a common record and genetic baseline for everyone to universally identify and understand how some diseases may be linked to genetics. Just as mathematics is a universal language, genetics could be this common language and record for human health.

---

32   "Keeping Up With Stem Cell Therapies. – Rising Tide Biology." 2020. Rising Tide Biology.

33   "DNA Sequencing Costs: Data." 2020. Genome.gov.

CHAPTER 2:

MEDICAL RECORDS AND THE NEED FOR A STREAMLINED SYSTEM

"The opportunity here is so much bigger than just electronic medical records. The opportunity is really to think in entirely new ways about how you do health care."[34]

–DR. BILL CROUNSE, SENIOR DIRECTOR OF
WORLDWIDE HEALTH FOR MICROSOFT

THE CASE FOR A STANDARDIZED MEDICAL RECORDS SYSTEM

The belief in proper medical documentation to improve patient care and outcomes dates back to the fifth century,

---

34 News, ABC. 2020. "President-Elect Urges Electronic Medical Records In 5 Years." ABC News.

BCE.[35] Hippocrates advocated for medical reporting, believing it served two goals: to reflect the course of the disease and indicate its causes. We have evidence of patient medical records dating back to ancient civilization, originally used for the physician's benefit.[36] The medical record told the story of a patient, which enabled the doctor to remember details that were easily lost or forgotten. In modern times, as specialization further diversifies health care, the need for records to facilitate cohesive care only increases.

Hippocrates' vision for a standard medical records system to streamline information between doctors and patients, unfortunately, isn't what we have today. Some healthcare providers still use paper charts. Some use one type of electronic medical records system whereas another hospital in the same city may use a different one. This makes a cohesive flow of information between systems very difficult.

Inconsistent medical records and the use of different documentation systems all contribute to inefficiencies across the healthcare system. This is one of the first challenges I've noted: we lack a standardized medical records system with streamlined information between health professionals that compiles all medical information for each patient in a universal electronic charting and evaluation system. This slows research and discovery and can hinder effective patient care. There are many reasons for this fragmentation in medical record keeping. Sometimes multiple companies operate different departments of the same hospital. Some departments

---

35 "Automating Medical Records In The 21St Century." 2020. Healthcareadministration.com.
36 "The Medical Record (R)Evolution." 2020. Forbes.com.

have acquired electronic medical record systems (EMRS), while others may still use paper. When visiting the same hospital but a different department, I often have to complete an entirely new set of paperwork.

A UNIVERSAL CHARTING SYSTEM AND PRECISION MEDICINE

However, I've begun to see a change at hospitals like Johns Hopkins, where I've been a patient for the last five years. During each visit, they take new pictures of my eyes and document the vision loss progression by reviewing a timeline of images and comparing this to the numerical measure of my vision. They can clearly observe changes in my eye health with thorough documentation under the same system, with the same procedures. Upon visiting another hospital, outside of the Johns Hopkins network, all of this information will have to be printed and sent in folders if the hospital doesn't have a compatible EMRS. What doctor will take the time to review five years' worth of medical records? Financially, they'll want to redo all imaging, using their own procedure and protocol. By streamlining hospitals onto the same EMRS or compatible versions, we can have a more accurate, complete, and precise history of the treatments a patient has received throughout their lives.

Without a streamlined system, much of our health information may be scattered across the country in warehouses, file cabinets, on servers, and in whatever cloud provider the hospital system uses. Artificial intelligence and machine learning cannot be applied to this information to detect patterns and "learn" across patient groups with the same diseases without a common system. The knowledge pool under which you are evaluated as a patient is limited to the doctors' recollection of their medical textbooks and other patients seen—not by an aggregated pool of thousands or millions of patients that could be used to find meaningful insights for treatment, outcomes, and key decisions about the future of our health.

I've tried taking medical documents from other hospitals to a new hospital. Most of the time, they don't accept them. They'll instead do new imaging and tests, even at facilities in different parts of the same city for a related visit, and for the same condition. This means less time for the patient to interact with the physician and other health care professionals, and too much time spent on administrative tasks that don't result in care delivery.

If multiple practitioners treat a patient, they need a common source to refer to and understand the findings of the other physicians' inpatient evaluation. One universal global metric could be a patient's genome if we continue making progress toward understanding how genomics influences health. Medical documentation increased in importance with the development of healthcare institutions in the nineteenth and twentieth centuries. While these records helped systematize patient care, they also aided in the transformation of medicine to the science that Hippocrates envisioned.

OUR CURRENT DISAGGREGATED MEDICAL RECORDS SYSTEM: THE PRICE OF INEFFICIENCY

Medical records took on new functions in the late twentieth century as the U.S. became more litigious.[37] Patient medical records became the basis of plaintiff claims in medical malpractice lawsuits and are, conversely, key evidence in justifying the physician's decision-making process. With the advent of Medicaid, Medicare, and private health insurance, billing and charting became intimately connected. More recently, medical records have become an integral part of the investigation and prosecution of fraudulent billing practices. Medical records are also now used by medical review boards to police the care quality physicians provide to patients.[38]

Many companies develop different EMRSs with incompatible software because all are competing for the same market share of sick patients and can charge higher premiums on the basis of more documentation. This inefficiency has a price. It costs doctors time, patients time, and money. It can also cost us our lives.

I accompanied my friend Francois (from France) to a U.S. hospital before his second surgery for the removal of a cancerous tumor (discussed at length in chapter 10). Providers gave him a pain injection and asked him to sign a waiver. They began filling out a paper binder of his information and were duplicating their own efforts by then typing this information into their system. The surgery started late because of

---

37   Evans, R. S. 2016. "Electronic Health Records: Then, Now, And In The Future." Yearbook Of Medical Informatics 25 (S 01): S48-S61. doi:10.15265/iys-2016-s006.

38   Ibid.

these administrative errors and a required protocol to have all patient information in the computer prior to beginning surgery.

Dissatisfied with what Francois considered a disorganized and highly overpriced system in the U.S., he turned to France for treatment. As his condition worsened and his surgeries didn't help, Francois revisited U.S. hospitals, but they were afraid and reluctant to treat him on the basis of what seemed like incomplete documentation because he'd had several procedures done in France. They were afraid of lawsuits and a potential medical liability, wasting Francois's time and delaying treatment.

Medical records and documentation not only aid physicians in patient evaluation and understanding disease progression, but they are also used as a means of billing patients for care.

The Affordable Care Act passed under the Obama Administration promoted the continuing development of EMRs to increase efficiencies and decrease costs. Health information technology was thus a necessary and sufficient condition for many of the ACA's initiatives.[39]

Sarah Fontenot holds a Bachelor of Science in Nursing, a law degree, and is currently a law professor. Teaching at Trinity University in San Antonio, Texas in the Department of Healthcare Administration, she writes, "On the cost reduction side, increased access to digital records will

---

39 Fontenot, Sarah. 2020. "The Affordable Care Act And Electronic Health Records. 2013. Ibid.

decrease costs, duplication and claim processing time by allowing multiple providers to rely upon one laboratory finding; by facilitating data mining to detect fraudulent billing practices; and by advancing per capita comparisons between communities with similar patients but disparate utilization rates."[39]

The rise of information technology influenced the belief in developing digital records. This way paper documents, if destroyed or lost, would no longer be an issue and patients could, in theory, one day access their entire medical history in a digital record.

Dr. David J. Brailer, the first national coordinator for health information technology, said, "The current information tools are still difficult to set up. They are hard to use. They fit only parts of what doctors do, and not the rest."[40]

But, in actual usage, they are a vehicle allowing physicians and other providers to create profuse notes on every patient encounter. The zeal for excessive documentation is not for the patient's benefit or the advancement of medical science; it is billing. The enormous, unintended consequence of EMRs is voluminous records overflowing with irrelevant information. The greatest concern about EMRs is also their greatest irony: the digital record that was supposed to increase communication in a patient's care has actually resulted in millions of computer-generated pages that no one ever reads.

---

40 "The Ups And Downs Of Electronic Medical Records | Medwrench." 2012. Medwrench.com.

MEDICAL DOCUMENTATION IMPROVEMENTS

Recent legislative requirements within our lifetime have also required an increase in patient documentation. This is supposed to capture the patient's medical history and every aspect of care they are receiving. We have increased the number of electronic medical devices for patient care but haven't yet fully linked these devices to automatically input patient information for doctors to review and interpret, rather than spending time recording it. An unstandardized approach to documentation across health care systems has led us to a less than complete and accurate picture upon a new patient visit.

I think this has also led to less precise medical evaluation, as the review generally narrows its focus to one part of the body that is injured, inflamed, etc., without evaluating the larger picture of other factors influencing health that may contribute to the disease or illness. The Obama Administration, as part of the Affordable Care Act, required health professionals to electronically document patients rather than continuing to use paper charts. This was an attempt to begin streamlining EMRs.

Creating a streamlined, interconnected EMR system across all U.S. hospitals could reduce inefficiencies and bring down the overall cost. It would also lead to the creation of a common data source or database from which we could, in theory, collectively learn more.

LOOKING AHEAD

Some countries in Europe are already beginning to streamline hospitals to use the same EMR. While I think every hospital could use their own system, I do think requiring compatible systems to streamline documentation will be helpful. Alternatively, storing patient data in the cloud with a unique identification code to access at each hospital with the patent's permission could be developed. This would enable access anywhere and in all hospitals with cloud access capabilities and a PIN login. This could lead to a more complete and precise medical history for patients. We are already starting to see big tech companies in partnerships with hospital systems to make this precise medical documentation more of a reality.

One baseline record between hospitals globally could be the human blueprint, or the genome, of each patient and its analysis to gain understanding and context for disease pre-disposition, risk factors, or potential to react to certain medications. The genome's language is the same, regardless of what dialect or system a hospital may use.

DIFFERENCES IN MEDICAL SOFTWARE PLATFORMS

In our current system, a patient's medical history throughout their lives is very often incomplete, particularly as they move. This results in duplicative data entry, repeated questioning during patient visits, and may even lead to misdiagnosis or mistreatment. Incomplete medical records and documentation not only hamper the potential treatment and outcome of a specific patient but also affect our own understanding and discovery of disease progression in other potential patients as we learn what does and doesn't work and why.

Particularly, in studying and understanding rare diseases, what causes them, and how to treat them, it is important to compare and compile information on patient treatments, outcomes, the disease's onset, and its progression. With our current model, this is difficult with millions of medical records unaligned between hospitals and doctors' offices across the country.

From 2015–2017, I experienced patient care in what the WHO ranks as the number one healthcare system in the world— France. I observed patient care in critical life conditions, out-patient home care, and what medical billing and pre- scription drug pricing were like. I met with Antoine Danchin, one of France's top scientists and a former researcher on the Human Genome Project. I spent three years with a French diplomat and scientific attaché to the U.S., Francois Gen- dre. As his English teacher, I saw Francois experience can- cer treatment both in the U.S. and in France and witnessed a different approach to medicine altogether. I realized that what we accept as standard care in the U.S. is not standard care in other countries, nor is it priced the same way.

Between my own experience as a patient with a rare genetic condition in the U.S. and experiencing a different form of care in the world's top-ranked healthcare system, I have compiled my experiences into an explanation of our current model: what it is, how it's changing, and how it can change for the better in the future. These changes are influencing a movement toward what some countries already have, such as a standardized EMRS.

Precision medicine and biotechnology are not only influenc- ing the ways in which we think about prescribing and deliv- ering care, but also how we pay for it. Rather than paying on the basis of medical services rendered, some companies and providers—influenced in part by the Affordable Care Act—adhere to a value-based payment model. In value-based care, a patient, in theory, pays on the basis of success in health outcomes from received medical services. This way, rather than incentivizing hospitals to render services with financial benefit to the system, more time can be focused on producing health outcomes and less time spent on considering treatment costs.

CONCLUSION

What I ascertained from doing this research is that our system, in its current model, cannot afford to keep itself afloat. Nor can government spending continue to cover what consumers cannot afford without adjustments. Creating a standard platform for EMRSs and a cloud bank to store/access health data can lead to more precise patient evaluation and diagnosis, more time with health care professionals, and less time doing administrative tasks. It might result in better, more precise, and affordable outcomes for patients. An integrated EMRS may also lead to less spending overall on our current model. It can also lead to more transparent care.

Precise treatments will initially be, and are, more expensive. But in the long term, costs will be reduced and patient outcomes will improve. The value of society's health and human longevity is priceless, and one we should and must invest in.

CHAPTER 3:

THE PRICE OF HEALTH AND OUR WILLINGNESS TO PAY

"Those of us with health insurance are also paying a hidden and growing tax for those without it – about $1000 per year that pays for somebody else's emergency room and charitable care."[41]

—*FORMER PRESIDENT BARACK OBAMA*

What are you willing to pay for your health, for your life, and for your family? For me, if there was treatment on the market today for Stargardt's, I would find a way to pay for it—whatever the price. Soon enough, I expect to find myself in this very position, with a potential treatment on the market that could improve my eyesight and my quality of life. The price tag for this will likely be in the millions of dollars.

---

41   "Obama's Health Care Speech To Congress." 2020. Nytimes.com

Gene therapies, CAR T-cell therapies, and other innovative treatments coming through the pipeline are so expensive that our health insurance system isn't designed to accommodate them.[42] Insurers will lose significant profits by covering the cost of million-dollar treatments per patient. So, for many, it comes down to the ability to pay out of pocket. Sometimes these innovative treatments are worth the price. That said, they beg the question of what price is fair for received outcomes.

The more I saw doctors after my diagnosis and was told there was nothing that could be done, the more I questioned what I was paying for. After visiting France and other countries, I realized we in the States pay more for health care than any other country worldwide.[43]

Total spending in the U.S. on healthcare averages three trillion dollars annually.[44] The U.S. spends more than two-and-a-half times than the U.K. and almost twice as much as Germany and Canada on healthcare. Median per capita spending among all Organization for Economic Development countries in 2009 was $3,223—less than half of the $7,960 per capita spent stateside.[45]

---

42 "CAR T-Cell Therapy: How Payers Are Responding To Huge Price Tags." 2020. Managed Healthcare Executive.

43 (US), National, Institute (US), Steven Woolf, and Laudan Aron. 2013. "Public Health And Medical Care Systems." National Academies Press (US).

44 Deloitte Health Outlook 2020.

45 US), National, Institute (US), Steven Woolf, and Laudan Aron. 2013. "Public Health And Medical Care Systems." National Academies Press (US).

When comparing the quality of our healthcare to other countries, the U.S. falls behind. In 2017, the U.S. was ranked thirty-seventh in the world for the quality of its healthcare system, behind Costa Rica, the Dominican Republic, Morocco, Saudi Arabia, Greece, Japan, and Singapore.[46] Some of the metrics used to determine overall quality were the health of a country's people, how a system responded to the level of health of its patients, and the distribution of "good health" (life expectancy, disease, and preventable disease rates), affordability of care delivered, and efficiency.[47]

Health system goals

	Level	Distribution	
Health	✔	✔	Efficiency
Responsiveness	✔	✔	
Fairness in financing		✔	
	Quality	Equity	

What we receive for what we pay doesn't always feel fair, accurate, or precise. Moreover, out-of-pocket spending across the country is on the rise.

---

46   Tandon, A. World Health Organization.*2020*. *Managing Overall Health System Performance for 191 Countries.*

47   US), National, Institute (US), Steven Woolf, and Laudan Aron. 2013. "Public Health And Medical Care Systems." National Academies Press (US).

PERPLEXING MEDICAL BILLS

In 2015, *Forbes* found that the cost of health care is rising higher than inflation.[48] It's difficult to pinpoint which areas in particular are on the rise. Medical invoices and billing are difficult to decipher—separating one cost from another is confusing not only for patients but also for hospitals. A study conducted at the University of Chicago found that 57 percent of American adults were surprised by a bill they thought would have been covered by medical insurance.[49] Survey participants said that 20 percent of their surprising medical bills were related to seeing a doctor out of network and not covered by their medical insurer.

"Most Americans have been surprised by medical bills that they expected would be covered by their insurance," said Caroline Pearson, senior fellow at NORC at the University of Chicago. "This suggests that consumers may have difficulty understanding their insurance benefits or knowing which providers are included in their plan's network."[50]

Inefficiencies in U.S. healthcare are no secret to those working within the system. According to one ER physician I spoke to, "A patient admitted to one hospital with a certain insurance may not be covered under the same insurance at a different hospital in the city."

---

48 "U.S. Health Care Costs Rise Faster Than Inflation." 2020. Forbes.com.

49 Ibid.

50 "New Survey Reveals 57 percent Of Americans Have Been Surprised By A Medical Bill | NORC.org." 2020. Norc.org.

THE UNEVEN COST OF HEALTH

What is the price of an ER physician for five minutes? Of having an X-Ray done? Of simply being admitted to the hospital? Of being given Tylenol in the ER? What is the price if you're rich or poor—with good insurance, average insurance, or no insurance at all?

When I see the doctor, I'm always trying to determine what level of care seems appropriate and what seems excessive. I once thought I had a retinal detachment and was concerned about traveling an hour and a half to see my primary ophthalmologist in Baltimore and taking time off from work. I called an ophthalmologist around the corner from my office to see if I could come in during my lunch break.

"I don't take insurance," he said. I froze and considered how much it could and should cost for him to tell me whether or not I had a retinal detachment. If detached, he would then refer me to an eye surgeon, without providing care himself. "How much?" I asked.

"$250 dollars."

I hung up and decided I'd save money by going to Baltimore, where at least I could anticipate a cheaper price with insurance.

A study done by the *Wall Street Journal* identified a hospital that was charging patients over $50,000 for knee replacement surgery.[51] The actual cost of performing the surgery at the hospital was between $7,500 and $10,500. Procedure

---

51   Sussman, Anna. 2020. "Burden Of Health-Care Costs Moves To The Middle Class." WSJ.

costs, of course, aren't revealed to patients beforehand. So what is reflected in the price tag post-surgery? What percentage is profit to the hospital at consumers' expense? According to one ER physician managing several hospital systems, the bulk of a hospital's profit is made on 6–10 percent of its patients. Most patients can't afford to pay their bills or don't have good insurance. To account for sunk costs, everyone is overcharged, and the highest costs are passed on to this wealthier bracket with the best insurance.

Price disparities aren't exclusive to surgeries and medical procedures. Another study in *The Atlantic* found large disparities in drug pricing between patients.[52] Should patients be charged $100,000, $200,000, or even $500,000 a year for drugs that aren't curative? Some say this is the fundamental challenge of a market-based healthcare system, which can deliver high-cost care with few alternatives for patients.

"No hospital system should be able to exercise market power to demand contract agreements that prevent more competitively priced networks," said Cigna's Chief Medical Officer, Alan Muney.[53]

Decisions for how to treat patients often come down to what insurance will cover. Indirectly, this also comes down to how much a patient is able to pay. Treatments can be so expensive that it isn't practical or affordable for an individual to pay out of pocket. A study in *The New England Journal of*

52   Emanuel, Ezekiel. 2019. "Big Pharma's Go-To Defense Of Soaring Drug Prices Doesn't Add Up." The Atlantic.

53   "Behind Your Rising Health-Care Bills: Secret Hospital Deals That Squelch Competition – WellNet Healthcare." 2018. WellNet Healthcare.

Medicine found that, on average, primary care physicians must address more than three dozen urgent uncompensated tasks every day—like discussing a patient's care plan with a specialist or working with a nurse to address the side effects of a patient's medication.[54]

And what exactly does access to care mean for individuals who are uninsured? According to the U.S. Census Bureau and the Kaiser Foundation, in 2012, almost forty-six million Americans were without health insurance, or nearly 15 percent of individuals under the age of sixty-five, which has increased since 2017.[55] With rising costs and a large uninsured population, it seems that many Americans will forgo medical care if they can avoid it for fear of the medical bills. A study done by the University of Chicago at the West Health Institute found that as many as 44 percent of Americans refuse medical care out of fear of the costs they will incur by seeking medical attention. About 40 percent of those surveyed said they also skipped a medical treatment or prescription for fear of the cost, even with insurance.

THE WORLD'S MOST EXPENSIVE HEALTH CARE IS BECOMING MORE EXPENSIVE

The demand for healthcare is on the rise globally with aging and growing populations, and so is the cost. Lower cost healthcare often means patients forgo seeking certain care altogether or choosing a medicine that the physician thinks

---

54 "What's Keeping Us So Busy In Primary Care? A Snapshot From One Practice | NEJM." 2020. New England Journal Of Medicine.
55 "Key Facts About The Uninsured Population." 2019. The Henry J. Kaiser Family Foundation.

won't be as effective as the newest, most effective treatments. When we seek healthcare, we generally really need it. Cost is always a concern, but our ability to understand or even question how we are being billed and what we are paying for is limited, as are our treatment options if we cannot afford them.

The expense of the U.S. healthcare system is a concern currently voiced by President Donald Trump as well as presidential candidates for the 2020 election. It has also been addressed under former President Obama's Affordable Care Act, and even under the Clinton Administration. Their concern for the rising cost of healthcare echoes the voices of millions of Americans struggling to access and pay for healthcare.

In 2017, the *Journal of the American Medical Association* reported that spending on healthcare in the U.S. between 1996 and 2015 rose by more than one trillion dollars.[56] The study examined five factors that it attributed to this increase— population growth, population aging, disease prevalence or inheritance, medical service utilization, and medial service price and intensity of the treatment (for example a broken leg cast as opposed to leg surgery). The researchers found that the factors of service price, intensity, and the rising cost of pharmaceutical drugs made up over 50 percent of this enormous increase in spending. According to the November 2013 issue of the journal, the primary reason for the rise in health care costs between 2000 and 2011—accounting for 91 percent—was an increase in the price of drugs, medical

---

56 "Why Do Healthcare Costs Keep Rising?" 2020. Investopedia.

devices, and hospital care.[57] At present, spending on health-care in the U.S. makes up more than 20 percent of GDP, a truly significant chunk of our economy.[58] Worldwide, health-care companies generate more profit annually in the U.S. than all other markets combined. Some argue we absorb the cost other governments are unwilling or unable to pay. As a reminder, the U.S. makes up around 4.3 percent of the world's population, which means we are paying far more for healthcare than the rest of the world.[59]

The laws of supply and demand tell us that the greater the demand for a good or service and the less the supply, the greater the price. In general, prices rise when demand increases relative to supply. Healthcare, in this case, may be no different. Other factors, such as political decisions about taxation rates, or increased regulation within the FDA for the approval of a new drug, can also influence health care costs. When the cost of health care increases, insurers raise premiums for consumers. They, too, have a bottom line.

57 Patton, Mike. 2020. "U.S. Health Care Costs Rise Faster Than Infla-tion." Forbes.

58 Ibid.

59 Patton, Mike. 2020. "U.S. Health Care Costs Rise Faster Than Infla-tion." Forbes.

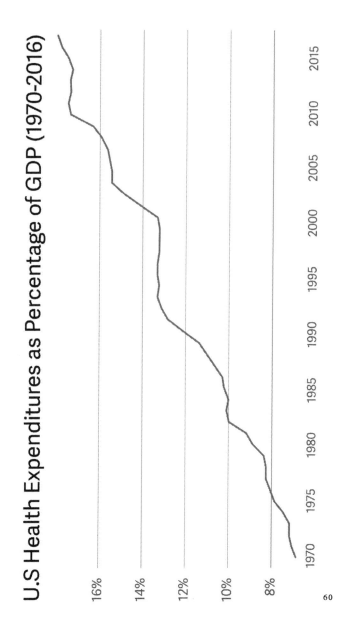

U.S Health Expenditures as Percentage of GDP (1970-2016)

60

60 "Why Do Healthcare Costs Keep Rising?" 2020. Investopedia.

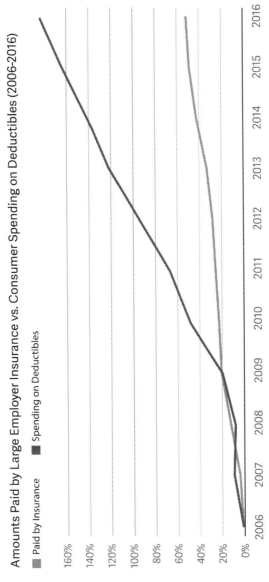

Cumulative Increase in Healthcare Costs

Amounts Paid by Large Employer Insurance vs. Consumer Spending on Deductibles (2006-2016)

■ Paid by Insurance   ■ Spending on Deductibles

160%
140%
120%
100%
80%
60%
40%
20%
0%

2006 2007 2008 2009 2010 2011 2012 2013 2014 2015 2016

61

61   "Why Do Healthcare Costs Keep Rising?" 2020. Investopedia.

HEALTH INSURANCE PREMIUMS AND OUT-OF-POCKET SPENDING ARE RISING

Increasing health care costs are being passed on to consumers in several ways. Average annual premiums for health insurance per U.S. family rose to $19,616, and in 2018, the average premium per individual with a private health insurance plan was $201.[62] What is clear is that at the time of the study, health care spending in several categories increased significantly. Where this cost must be absorbed is on the consumer and the insurers (whether private providers or the government). While government policy and lifestyle changes were also cited as reasons for increases in health insurance costs to consumers, the more plausible explanation seems to be the overall increase in health care services across the board in a variety of sectors.

Nearly half of Americans have a chronic illness diagnosed by a medical physician.[63] Government services such as Medicaid and Medicare have increased accessibility to medical services, thus enabling a higher demand for medical services by consumers. An increase in demand with a short labor supply can be correlated with an increase in price for medical services. [64]

Between 2006 and 2016, the cost of out-of-pocket expenses for Americans rose faster than costs covered by insurance

---

62   Sussman, Anna. 2020. "Burden Of Health-Care Costs Moves To The Middle Class." WSJ.

63   Century, Institute. 2002. "The Health Care Delivery System." National Academies Press (US).

64   Ibid.

companies. The deductible average out-of-pocket annual medical expense per American family is $13,300.[65]

HOSPITALS HAVE BARGAINING POWER

Two patients receiving the same treatment or procedure, such as a broken ankle at the same hospital and under the care of the same physician, nevertheless may receive very different bills. An emergency room medical physician in West Virginia described it as negotiation in the medical billing process. "It's why Tylenol in the ER costs $500—a hospital knows they are going to lose money treating certain patients with low-quality insurance, or with no insurance, but are obligated to treat them. That sunk cost is passed on to a patient with good insurance who can pay, for the same service and treatment. We know the patient and the insurer may pay a percentage of the bill, but not all of it. So we overbill and hope that they can pay."

According to *The Washington Post,* joint replacements are the most common hospital procedure for Medicare patients. Prices ranged from a low of $5,304 in Ada, Oklahoma, to $223,373 in Monterey Park, California. The average charge across the Medicare patients' joint replacements was $52,063.[66]

"It's true that Medicare and a lot of private insurers never pay the full charge," said Renee Hsia, an assistant professor at the

---

65 Sussman, Anna. 2020. "Burden Of Health-Care Costs Moves To The Middle Class." WSJ.

66 Kliff, Sarah. 2013. One hospital charges $8,000 — another, $38,000. *Washington Post.*

University of California, San Francisco School of Medicine. Her research focuses on price variation. "But you have a lot of private insurance companies where the consumer pays a portion of the charge. For uninsured patients, they face the full bill. In that sense, the price matters."[67]

Some experts attribute the disparities to a health system that can set prices with impunity because consumers rarely see them—and rarely shop for discounts.

In 2010, the year the Affordable Care Act passed, the annual number of hospital mergers shot up from 40 to 59 percent, and the number of deals has remained above sixty every year since, according to Irving Levin Associates, a research firm that tracks healthcare transactions.[68] Hospital systems are trying to realize efficiencies and savings through increased Mergers and Acquisitions (M&A) activity—but so far, prices haven't dropped."[69]

"Part of the reason we spend more on health care each year is the nation's growing and aging population," said Dr. Joseph Dieleman of the Institute for Health Metrics and Evaluation at the University of Washington and lead author of the study. "But factors relating to the health system, such as increased price, intensity, and utilization, are driving most of the spending increase."

---

67   Ibid.
68   Behind Your Rising Health-Care Bills: Secret Hospital Deals That Squelch Competition – WellNet Healthcare." 2018. WellNet Healthcare.
69   Kliff, Sarah. 2013. One hospital charges $8,000 — another, $38,000. *Washington Post*.

"When we added up the bill, the health conditions, increasing population size led to a 23 percent increase in health care spending," Dr. Dieleman said. "People are getting older led to a 12 percent increase in spending, and increases in price and service intensity, that is the variety and complexity of services, led to a 50 percent increase in spending."[70]

Some of the most interesting insights from the study, however, suggest how and why we pay so much for health care, and in what stage of our lives.

"These findings offer insight into why the U.S. spends so much on health care," said Dr. Jay Want, Executive Director of the Peterson Center on Healthcare. "Increased health care spending is driven more by how care is priced and delivered to patients than by the population's size or age. The research suggests the need for more efforts to address those forces that control pricing."[71]

Many people believe the Department of Defense has the largest budget of a federal agency fueled by tax dollars. The Department of Health and Human Services, however, covering Medicaid and Medicare, has the largest federal budget: nearly double the DoD's annual spending at over one trillion dollars annually.[72]

---

70 "New Study Explains Why US Health Care Spending Increased $1 Trillion." 2017. Institute For Health Metrics And Evaluation.
71 "New Study Explains Why US Health Care Spending Increased $1 Trillion." 2017. Institute For Health Metrics And Evaluation.
72 "2019 U.S. Federal Budget Spending by Agency." Usaspending.gov

OUR MARKET-DRIVEN MODEL IS REALLY A SHARED MODEL

While our current healthcare system is understood and por-trayed as being a capitalistic, free-market model, this is far from precise. The expense has risen for everyone, despite our private and public insurance market-based model. The system, as it is, cannot afford to pay for itself. The cost to pay for everyone is passed on to the consumers that can afford to pay more, rather than everyone paying a flat, or relatively standard, rate. So if I'm a patient going to a hospital with good insurance, and you don't have good insurance and can-not afford to pay out of pocket for your treatment, the cost is passed on to me. Ultimately, I'm given a higher bill for the same procedure.

The question of who should pay and how the cost should be distributed across socio-economic classes has shifted. In the last decade, the U.S. government has increased its spending on healthcare as the average age in the U.S. has increased and more people are on Medicare benefits. The ACA expanded medical benefits for individuals on Medicaid and provided subsidies for low-income Americans buying insurance on state exchanges. Middle-class Americans are also paying more out of pocket for medical care.[73]

Harvard health care economist Dr. David Cutler calls this the "story of three Americas." One group, the wealthiest, can afford health care relatively easily. On average, the poorest parts of society rely on public assistance programs, and the

---

73 Sussman, Anna. 2020. "Burden Of Health-Care Costs Moves To The Middle Class." WSJ.

lower-middle to middle-class income struggle with rising health care costs. In 2014, seven years after the recession, Brookings Institute Senior Fellow Diane Schanzenbach found that middle-income households' healthcare spending was 25 percent higher than spending before the recession, even as spending fell for other "basic needs" such as food, housing, clothing, and transportation.[74]

Employers still typically pay roughly 80 percent of individual health insurance premiums, a share that has held fairly steady in the past five years, thanks in part to changing plan designs that shift more costs to workers, said Beth Umland, director of research on health and benefits at Mercer US. Moreover, the Kaiser Family Foundation found deductibles for individual workers have soared in the past five years, rising 67 percent since 2010 without adjusting for inflation—roughly seven times earnings growth over the same period. [75]

VALUE-BASED CARE MAY BE MORE PRECISE

In 2015, the Obama Administration began to address increasing costs in relation to quality in healthcare and introduced a new payment model.[76] The Administration attempted to move healthcare toward a value-based model with a timeline and a set of metrics to accomplish this. This reform attempted to address the incentives to deliver quality care to patients rather than providing services. By treating patients

---

74 Ibid.
75 Sussman, Anna. 2020. "Burden Of Health-Care Costs Moves To The Middle Class." WSJ
76 "Building A System That Works: The Future Of Health Care | Health Affairs." 2020. Healthaffairs.org.

on the basis of services rather than outcomes, hospitals are financially incentivized to deliver more services, perform more imaging, and provide extra care that may not provide better outcomes or deliver higher-quality care. Whether or not we admit it, healthcare is an enormous business that has profit motives like any other industry, only with more certain and steady cash flows in the business of certain illnesses and finite existences.

WHY COLLECTIVELY INVEST IN A SHARED, STREAMLINED SYSTEM WITH A VALUE-BASED MODEL?

In the previous chapter, I outlined some of the efficiencies and cost savings that could be realized with a streamlined, interconnected EMRS paired with the genome of each patient, and the application of AI to aggregated data sets to help physicians make treatment recommendations. Such a system could also schematize the medical billing process, increase transparency for patients, and potentially decrease total spend. It could also realign incentives for hospital systems to deliver value-based care to patients if the financial incentive is better outcomes, as opposed to more care.

Precision medicine treatments like gene therapies and CAR T-cell therapies are already on the market and are so highly priced that only the wealthiest can generally afford them. Currently, prescription drug prices are estimated to make up 10 percent of national health spending in the U.S.[77]

---

77 Sussman, Anna. 2020. "Burden Of Health-Care Costs Moves To The Middle Class." WSJ.

Some of these prescription treatments could be replaced by more precise medicines, with fewer side effects and more targeted outcomes. If we choose to invest in their continued research and development, we may just find a way to bring the cost down for everyone, as well as improving our own health and quality and longevity of life as a society.

CHAPTER 4:

THE DRUG DEVELOPMENT PIPELINE AND THE COST TO INNOVATE

———

"Wherever the art of medicine is loved, there is also a love of humanity."

−HIPPOCRATES

MY EXPERIENCE WITH CLINICAL TRIALS

When I was freshly returned from Peace Corps service, my grandmother decided I was ready to volunteer myself to science. A veteran and retired Air Force nurse, she dutifully handed me an article in *Time* magazine featuring a twenty-eight-year-old receiving stem cell injections to treat

Stargardt's.[78] The stem cells became new photoreceptors, restoring his vision. "This is going to be *very* expensive—it might be easier to access through a clinical trial," she said. "You're young, no health problems, no medications—you're a perfect candidate."

Johns Hopkins and Wills Eye Institute evaluated me for clinical trials. The requirements were rigorous: regular stem cell eye injections, immune suppressant drugs, no medications for the study's duration, and frequent check-ups for several years. After my evaluation, however, the doctors declared my Stargardt's too mild; I didn't make the cut. "Let's wait until this is in phase three or on the market—focus on preserving your vision for now," they said. I was afraid but definitely impatient. I knew my vision was declining and walked away knowing that progress could take decades. But I also left with newfound knowledge about the time, expense, regulation, and meticulous work that goes into developing drugs. More often than not, new drugs don't even make it through all clinical trials.

CURRENT STATE: DRUG PRICING AND THE COST TO INNOVATE

Drug development is a risky business. Ask anyone in the industry and they'll tell you about the low probability of a return on investment. "Only one out of every 12.5 potential drugs ever reaches patients.[79] The average drug takes eleven

---

78 Park, Alice. 2014. "Stem Cells Allow Nearly Blind Patient to See." *Time.*
79 DiMasi, Joseph A, Ronald W Hansen, and Henry G Grabowski. 2003. "The Price Of Innovation: New Estimates Of Drug Development Costs." Journal Of Health Economics 22 (2): 151-185. doi:10.1016/s0167-6296(02)00126-1.

to fourteen years to develop, and the costs of bringing a drug to market range from $1 to $2.6 billion," wrote Anupam Jena, professor of health care policy at Harvard Medical School.[80]

Ronald Pepin, a PhD biologist, is senior Vice President and Chief Business Officer at Celldex Therapeutics. He has spent his career developing new cancer drugs and hasn't lost hope. I spoke to him on drug development processes. "You're looking at less than a 5 percent chance of success of clearing FDA trials I, II, and III and bringing a new drug to market. For cancer therapies, the probability of success is even less," said Ronald.

"Can we really put a price on a better, longer life?" I asked. Ronald agreed.

I also spoke to Annette Grimaldi, a career investment banker at BMO Capital Markets in New York City. Annette connects pharmaceutical and biotech companies to investors, helping them determine which products are likely to succeed. Specifically, I asked why she's in this risky investment business of new drugs and healthcare. While she thinks the rising cost of drug development isn't sustainable, she also believes in taking the risk for the sake of humanity.

"Time to market after the initial investment is typically ten to fifteen years," said Annette. "Most investors aren't interested in that." Imagine investing $100 million in a new product

80   DiMasi, Joseph A., Henry G. Grabowski, and Ronald W. Hansen. 2016. "Innovation In The Pharmaceutical Industry: New Estimates Of R&D Costs." Journal Of Health Economics 47: 20-33. doi:10.1016/j.jhealeco.2016.01.012.

without seeing any returns for ten years or more and imagine your 5 percent chance of making it through all clinical trials. If it makes it, your returns may be huge, and you can think about saving people's lives and may be set for retirement and exotic vacations. If your product fails, you may be broke and have to wait ten years to realize you won't see any returns.

Pharmaceutical companies argue that maintaining high pricing helps them continue innovating, researching, and developing new drugs. The intellectual patent and monopoly, some argue, is the reward. Others argue that IP protection is becoming outdated, and the rewards now outweigh the costs to consumers. To pharmaceutical companies, that is the cost to innovate life-saving products. PhD geneticist Victor Li thinks these strong returns are a motivating factor for innovation. Without the protection of intellectual property and patents, or the chance of enormous payoffs, people have fewer incentives to develop new drugs. "I was born and raised in China, where intellectual patent laws were not developed until the 1980s. Now, biotech investing is booming in China," said Victor.

As an inventor, Victor immigrated to the U.S. and generated wealth as an inventor and entrepreneur, first working on the Human Genome Project, then launching his own endeavors. Victor holds over sixty patents, ranging from biomedical deceives to new ideas for pharmaceutical treatments. Now, he's in the investment business with the scientific wherewithal to think through whether or not a new medical product is likely to succeed. Victor thinks that too much pricing control leaves fewer incentives or rewards for people to constantly innovate. "Too much price control may dampen the enthusiasm of biotech investors. In a touch industry like biopharma, enormous financial payoffs are tough to keep driving the industry and research forward."

THE PROBLEM: U.S. PHARMACEUTICALS ARE THE MOST EXPENSIVE IN THE WORLD

As previously stated, Americans pay more for healthcare and drugs than the rest of the world. Francois Gendre, a molecular biologist and diplomat at the French Embassy in Washington D.C. termed the U.S. drug pricing system absurd. "You pay a hundred times the price for a drug here compared to France," he said. "This cannot be sustained." A study conducted by the Johns Hopkins School of Public Health found that U.S. prescription drug prices for brand-name drugs are the world's highest. While volume is sold internationally, the bulk of pharmaceutical revenues are made in the U.S., which holds over 45 percent of the world's pharmaceutical market—a total market share of $446 billion in 2016.[81] And prices are on the rise. "Every year we pay more for brand-name drugs and other countries pay less for the same drugs," said Gerard Anderson, professor in the Johns Hopkins Department of Health Policy. U.S. consumers on average pay three to four times as much as Japan, the U.K., and Canada for the same product. Anderson also found significant variation in price differentials between the U.S. and its foreign counterparts. For some drugs, the price was 30 percent higher in the U.S., while other drugs were 7,000 percent more expensive.[82]

---

81 "Topic: Pharmaceutical Industry In The U.S.." 2020. Www.Statista.com.
82 "Report Shows US Brand-Name Drug Prices 'Highest In The World'."
    2019. European Pharmaceutical Review.

What's also concerning is that incentives to develop treatments for rare diseases don't seem to be working, despite government funding and subsidies existing to fund this research. Research and development costs are high for any new drug in the U.S., and if you're treating a small group of people, your chances of reaping financial returns decrease. Why invest in an expensive and slow process for patients making up less than 1 percent of the population, knowing that most of them might not have good insurance? Now consider the number of disqualifying factors in conducting a clinical trial: other health issues, being on medication, being pregnant, or not having the time to commit to a voluntary study over the several years of medical testing and evaluation.

Remember, hospitals often make their profits from the 6 to 7 percent of the population with good insurance plans. As a physician, you may be unlikely to prescribe a drug not covered by insurance or one that is too expensive for the patient. So as a patient with Stargardt's, which affects one in 20,000 people, I think that financial incentives for a cure are low or not effectively offset by government subsidies—unless the new drug has an overlapping application for a larger disease group. Luckily, macular degeneration treatments are similar to Stargardt's patients, and MD patients make up a whopping 12.5 percent of adults over sixty, and 30 percent of adults over eighty—enough people to be profitable.[83] And luckily, some stem cell and gene therapy mechanisms could be applied the same way to people with different diseases.

---

83 "Age-Related Macular Degeneration (AMD) Data And Statistics | National Eye Institute." 2020. Nei.Nih.gov.

As a consumer, you might ask why pharmaceutical giants can exercise so much pricing power over U.S. consumers and charge more than they would in France. Part of the explanation lies in the uncertain, slow, heavily regulated process of drug development.

THE DRUG DEVELOPMENT PIPELINE IN THE U.S.

I interviewed an employee at the U.S. FDA to get a better understanding of the drug development process. The FDA's regulation of medical devices, drugs, and biologics is very different and has increased in complexity with more technology and more products. Pharmaceuticals require an investigation, new trial application, and clinical protocol before beginning human experimentation. Some criteria evaluated before trials I, II, and III begin are:

- How you'll monitor patients
- Data collection methods
- Robustness of the study
- Data analysis methodology
- How and where you manufactured the drug
- Expiration of the drug

After making it through all three trials, a drug can have patent protection to prevent other companies from manufacturing it. This enables them to reduce competition until the patent expires. The FDA doesn't have the authority to regulate drug prices or consider drug pricing in the approval process. The U.S. Patent and Trademark Office is responsible for issuing patents; the FDA plays a ministerial role here, and a drug doesn't need FDA approval to receive patent protection. However, the FDA cannot grant a generic drug approval that is subject to exclusivities.

In contrast to the U.S., regulatory bodies in the European Union dictate what pharmaceutical companies can charge. Twenty-nine European countries—as well as Australia, New Zealand, Brazil, and South Africa—use this approach for the purposes of setting and negotiating the price of a drug.[84] This controls and protects consumers from overpaying, or paying unfair prices for health, which generics in the U.S. have helped.

LESS EXPENSIVE OPTIONS: GENERICS

The Hatch-Waxman Act from 1984 was important for the development of cost-effective health options for Americans: generic drugs.[85] Before obtaining new drug application approval, the company owns the intellectual rights to all the information in the New Drug Application (NDA). If a company did all the testing in the drug, then all the data is owned by the company. Historically, it was difficult to develop generics, as companies couldn't reference and access data from another company's drug patent.

Now, generic drug developers have the right to reference data submitted in an NDA. They can submit an application with limited clinical data without having to do a full-blown clinical trial instead of referencing an already approved drug in support of their generic drug application. Another fast track

---

84 "Report Shows US Brand-Name Drug Prices 'Highest In The World'." 2019. European Pharmaceutical Review.
85 "What Is Hatch-Waxman?" 2020. Phrma.org.

to navigating the FDA approval process is a voucher in which the review period is shorter for a new drug.

BIOLOGICS ARE THE FUTURE BUT ARE MORE EXPENSIVE

Unlike a drug, which is a chemical entity or molecule, a biologic is generally a protein-based therapy that could be an enzyme (like insulin), or an antibody.[86] Biologics are more complex than a chemical entity and cannot be replicated as easily as chemically based generics (termed biosimilars). With more variability in biologics, regulation is different. Increasingly, drug developers are focusing on biologics like cellular therapies, gene therapies, and stem cell therapies. These represent the transition from pharmaceuticals to biopharmaceuticals. "The trend we are seeing is the development of more biotherapies, a departure from traditional chemical-based therapies," said U.S. Ambassador Robert Cekuta, who served as ambassador and chief economic affairs officer in Azerbaijan, Japan, Germany, and other counties.

In part due to their newness and variability, biologics are more expensive. Moreover, production and manufacturing are very different processes. Think of large-scale production facilities harvesting and growing cells (detailed in Chapter 14). Instead of chemically engineering molecules to create a non-living, predictable chemical reaction, we have bioengineers growing and harvesting cells. Life is creative, chaotic, and unpredictable—in other words, it's hard to engineer.

---

86 THOMAS MORROW, Linda Hull Felcone. 2004. "Defining The Difference: What Makes Biologics Unique." Biotechnology Healthcare 1 (4): 24.

Our ability to engineer biologics with machines is clumsy compared to the natural mechanisms of cells producing them.

CONCLUSION

Continuing innovation in new drugs while ensuring they're affordable and accessible will be increasingly significant in the precision medicine era. An advantage this type of medicine presents is enabling researchers to more precisely identify patient populations to conduct trials on (rather than random subjects). Ultimately, a multi-faceted approach among governments, educators, society, pharmaceutical companies, and business leaders is needed to achieve our "health shot."

What if, rather than looking at new drug investments as a financial payoff, we look at it as an investment in the betterment of humanity, with *some* financial returns? I believe there can be a compromise, and better treatment options can be made more affordable with precision medicine and technology if we collectively agree to invest in them for humanity. We need to become smarter as consumers and developers. Francois, Victor, and Annette have invested in the biopharma future. The three breakthroughs I'll discuss in Part 2 can take us there.

PART 2:

THREE BREAKTHROUGHS DRIVING PRECISION MEDICINE'S PROGRESS

CHAPTER 5:

MAPPING THE HUMAN BLUEPRINT AND THE GENE SEQUENCING REVOLUTION

———

"All the main domains of science have evolved from a starting point where a particular area of the physical world was subjected to some kind of classification, taxonomy, or system."
—ANTOINE DANCHIN

Can the human genome be used as a lens through which we try to understand and approach healthcare treatment and disease diagnosis today? This is an approach some companies and health professions are taking as they develop new medicines, diagnose and treat disease, and think about the future of healthcare. Some health professionals believe this can solve some of the challenges outlined in the previous chapter and eventually help make treatment and diagnosis of disease more precise, effective, affordable, and efficient. Within the last few decades alone, we've made significant progress in genetics. To understand this progression, this chapter will start from historical beginnings.

WHERE WE STARTED

Half a century ago, little was understood about genetic factors in human disease. In 1953, Rosalind Franklin, James Watson, and Francis Crick described the double helix structure of deoxyribonucleic acid, or DNA, as the genetic instructions for building, running, and maintaining living organisms.[87]

While there are billions of cells in every human body, nearly every cell has the same DNA. Most DNA is located in the nucleus of the cell and some in the mitochondria. Information stored in DNA is a code made of up four chemical bases: adenine, guanine, cytosine, and thymine. Think of these as base pairs that make up gene sequences, like computer language of binary code composed of ones and zeros. Instead of two numbers, DNA sequences have four bases, or numbers, that always pair with one another.[88] Human DNA consists of three billion bases.[89]

While this sounds like an abundance of possible sequences that can create an almost limitless variety of combinations, approximately 99 percent of these sequences are the same across all people. The sequence of these bases

---

87 "Francis Crick." 2020. Profiles In Science.

88 Ibid.

89 Reference, Genetics. 2020. "What Is DNA?" Genetics Home Reference

determines the information available for building and maintaining an organism. This is similar to the way in which letters of the alphabet appear in a certain order to form words and sentences. DNA base sequences pair together, A to T and C to G. With a sugar phosphate bond, these base pairs form nucleotides and make up what we have come to know as the double helix (RNA, by contrast, is a single helix). It wasn't until our lifetime, however, that we had an entire human genome sequenced to begin interpreting what the 1 percent difference in genetic makeup between people even means.[90]

THE HUMAN GENOME PROJECT

In 1990, an international concerted effort began to sequence the three billion genes, or base pairs, in the human genome. This was the Human Genome Project. The goal was to provide researchers with tools to understand the genetic factors in human disease. Spanning thirteen years, with its completion in 2003, the project sparked a revolution in the global biotechnology community.[91]

When the Human Genome Project began, sequencing technology was in its infancy. Much of the sequencing was done manually. Much of their work was looking at images of DNA sequencing, and copying them, like copying a book, by hand. The eventual application of computers and sequencing technology moved the project forward and made the information useful and digestible, enabling researches to make

---

90 "Francis Crick." 2020. Profiles In Science.
91 Ibid.

meaningful conclusions from the tremendous amount of data within every genome.[92]

Since mapping the genome, we have discovered over 1,800 disease-causing genes. Having the complete sequence of the human genome is like having the blueprint for an automobile. The sequences are pages of a manual for how the human body works. Having the human genome mapped—the initial blueprint—is only the beginning. Today's challenge is to determine how to read the contents of these pages and understand how all of these many, complex parts work together in human health and disease. "Sequencing the human genome is only the first step, but it is the most important step," said Victor Li of Human Genome Sciences. As a reminder, Dr. Li was one researcher on the Human Genome Project. "The DNA blueprint is the primary structure. Then we have secondary, tertiary and additional structures that build upon this—we are only at the beginning of understanding what it all means."

The progress we've made, and are continuing to make, is inspiring and helps push the movement for more precise medicine forward. It has also influenced a whole new generation of scientists, engineers, entrepreneurs, lawyers, and physicians.

KEY LESSONS FROM THE HUMAN GENOME PROJECT

What we can learn from the Human Genome project—beyond decoding the genome and having this blueprint—is

---

92   Ibid.

the importance of cross-disciplinary thinking. "Genomics brought the idea of team science and collaboration to biology," said Carlos Bustamante, professor of genetics at Stanford. Today's biology brings together people with backgrounds in ethics, computer science, physics, chemistry, healthcare, art, and mathematics, among other disciplines. At the onset of the project, many biologists failed to see the implications of mapping the genome for science and medicine.

Scientists are notorious for being intensely competitive and wanting to make independent discoveries. They often compete for funding, resources, and publication. This individual perspective, however, no longer fits in the genomics era of collective, collaborative thinking. By sharing discoveries, we can challenge one another and build upon the original idea.

Under the direction of Dr. James Watson, a consortium of scientists from around the world gathered in 1990 with the objective of decoding the human genome. "One of James Watson's motivations was to bring together the best and the brightest from many different disciplines—not only biology but physics, chemistry, engineering—all of this would have to get together for this to work," said Francis Collins, Director at the National Human Genome Research Institute.[93]

Talent and bright ideas can come from anywhere. For the Human Genome Project to be completed, it required cross-disciplinary thinking and international collaboration

---

93   Lessons from the Human Genome Project. 2018.

and providing some of the best thinkers with the tools and opportunity to contribute. Many of the world's participants in the project didn't move to participate but worked from different countries around the world. [94]

While the Human Genome Project was extensive in scope, expensive, and took considerable effort, the outcome has given us a path forward. The effort also demonstrated to the scientific community and signaled to the world the importance of large-scale scientific collaborative efforts. Efforts like this will be essential to continue improving our medical health systems and drug development forward. It reminds us of the universality of genetics and what it may mean for improving health outcomes. After all, "There's no partisan difference in people wanting to live as long as they can," said former President Bill Clinton.[95]

The Human Genome Project also influenced contemporary views of data sharing. Scientists quickly realized that by sharing information between different parts of the genome, they could make more meaningful conclusions. Sharing this data means more than being able to make conclusions about what the human genome means—it also means sharing information that can make a life or death difference.

Information we can pull from patients' genomes is information we can and will use for centuries to advance our understanding of human health. The more genomes we have sequenced and the more we share this information, the faster

---

94 Ibid.
95 Ibid.

we can make discoveries, improve medical care, and have a better understanding of how life works and how and why disease occurs.

A NEW GENERATION OF GENETICS

Today, many patients express fear and hesitation at having their genomes sequenced. They are concerned that the information will be used in some way against them. In addition to including scientists and engineers in the Human Genome Project, geneticists, social scientists, and lawyers were also included to discuss potential ethical issues and societal concerns. An entirely new generation of scientists left the project with these considerations in mind.[96]

What the Human Genome project taught is the importance of being bold and courageous as we step forward in unraveling and understanding. It's also taught us that we are only at the beginning; we will have to be realistic about the progress we will make, but we have to try. Many scientists speculate that once we start using genomic information as a routine part of patient care, we will begin making the most significant progress.

This genomic information is currently being applied to patients with diseases like cancer, rare genetic disorders, hypertension, diabetes, and Alzheimer's. As we learn more, we apply it to patients with all kinds of conditions and have a better understanding of how they will react to certain medicines and what their best course of treatment is.

96 Lessons from the Human Genome Project. 2018.

"I dream of the day when every young mother brings a young child home from the hospital with a little gene card that says, 'This is the way you should prepare this child's healthcare,'" said former President Bill Clinton.[97]

GENOMIC SEQUENCING CREATES NEW BUSINESS MODELS

Beyond reshaping biology, the discovery of the double helix is reshaping business. Today, the U.S. invests more money in biotechnology research and development and biopharmaceutical industries than anywhere else in the world.[98] As we pool our efforts, discoveries, and knowledge together globally, we step closer every day to understanding what makes us human. In clinical applications, we are working on treatments for previously "untreatable" illnesses. [99]

Based on a deeper understanding of disease at the genomic level, we are beginning to see a whole new generation of targeted interventions. Many of these will be much more effective and (hopefully) have fewer side effects than those on the market today. Today, developing a new drug isn't as simple as creating a pill that is semi-effective and safe for the masses—it's about developing precise, targeted, and highly effective treatments for specific population groups. Rather than blockbuster drugs for the masses, the financial incentive will be for a precise treatment for specific patients that work and align with "value-based care." Companies like Bristol

---

97 Ibid.
98 "Take A Look At Ranking Of The Top Biotech Countries In The World." 2020. The Balance.
99 Ibid.

Myers Squibb and AstraZeneca have realized this and have transitioned from being traditional pharmaceutical firms to biopharmaceuticals that are more agile in design, idea generation, and use data throughout drug development processes to adjust manufacturing.

Bill Clinton's dream is being realized. Over the past twenty years, our ability to understand and engineer complex and precise genetic circuits has outpaced scientific discovery. Several factors have contributed to this progress. Today, sequencing thousands of genomes from which we can now "mine" genes is more possible than ever before. We've developed efficient and cost-effective methods of sequencing and synthesizing DNA, and this way have an improved understanding of biophysics to enable simulations of the genome.[100]

Companies are working to make genome sequencing a new standard of care for all patients. And some are doing it in a cost-effective, efficient, sustainable way. Here is an overview of the progress companies have driven forward in sequencing technology, and how they've made it economical.

---

100 Lessons from the Human Genome Project. 2018.

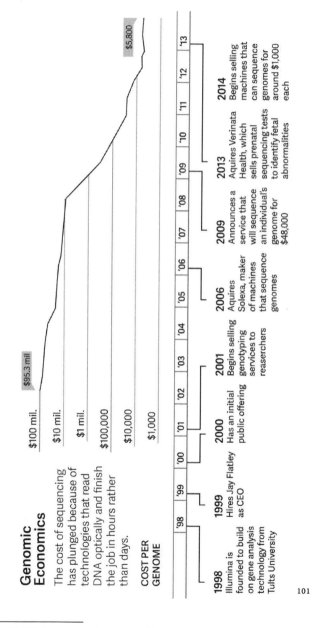

Genomic Economics

The cost of sequencing has plunged because of technologies that read DNA optically and finish the job in hours rather than days.

COST PER GENOME

$100 mil. $95.3 mil
$10 mil.
$1 mil.
$100,000
$10,000 $5,800
$1,000

'98 '99 '00 '01 '02 '03 '04 '05 '06 '07 '08 '09 '10 '11 '12 '13

1998
Illumina is founded to build on gene analysis technology from Tufts University

1999
Hires Jay Flatley as CEO

2000
Has an initial public offering

2001
Begins selling genotyping services to reaserchers

2006
Aquires Solexa, maker of machines that sequence genomes

2009
Announces a service that will sequence an individual's genome for $48,000

2013
Aquires Verinata Health, which sells prenatal sequencing tests to identify fetal abnormalities

2014
Begins selling machines that can sequence genomes for around $1,000 each

101

101 "DNA Sequencing Costs: Data." 2020. Genome.gov.

HOW GENE SEQUENCING WORKS

At 23andMe, consumers can easily order a genomic test. Using the contents of a saliva kit, they mail in a saliva sample. The DNA is then amplified from the sample and extracted so there is enough to be genotyped. The DNA is then cut into small pieces and applied to a glass microarray chip, which has many microscopic beads applied to its surface.[102] Each bead has a probe that matches the DNA of one of the many variants the company tests for. If the sample has a match in the microarray, the sequences will hybridize or bind together, letting researchers know that this variant is present in the customer's genome by a fluorescent label coated on the probes. Tens of thousands of variants are tested out of the ten to thirty million located in the entire genome.[103] These matches are then compiled into a report that is supplied to the customer, allowing them to know if the variants associated with certain diseases—such as Parkinson's, celiac, and Alzheimer's—are present in their own genome.

Uninterpreted raw genetic data may then be downloaded by customers. This provides customers with the ability to choose one of the twenty-three chromosomes, as well as mitochondrial DNA, to see which base is located in certain positions in genes and see how these compare to other common variants.[104]

---

102 Dr. Leming Shi, National Center for Toxicological Research. "MicroArray Quality Control (MAQC) Project". U.S. Food and Drug Administration. Retrieved 2007-12-26.

103 Ibid.

104 Dr. Leming Shi, National Center for Toxicological Research. "MicroArray Quality Control (MAQC) Project". U.S. Food and Drug Administration. Retrieved 2007-12-26.

Customers who bought tests with an ancestry-related component have online access to genealogical DNA test results and tools, including a relative-matching database.[105] Customers can also view their maternal mitochondrial haplogroup and, if they are male or a relative shared a patriline that has also been tested, Y chromosome paternal haplogroup.[106] U.S. customers who bought tests with a health-related component and received health-related results before November 22, 2013 have online access to an assessment of inherited traits and genetic disorder risks. Health-related results for U.S. customers who purchased the test from November 22, 2013 onwards were suspended until late 2015, while the process underwent an FDA regulatory review.[107] Customers who bought tests from 23andMe's Canadian and U.K. locations have access to some, but not all, health-related results. As of February 2018, 23andMe had genotyped over 3,000,000 individuals.[108] 23andMe has made genomic sequencing easy, cost-effective, efficient, and very popular nationwide.

One of the challenges of the Human Genome Project was the time it took to sequence a single genome (over a decade), and the expense (over three billion USD). Cost and time, then, were recently prohibitive for globally scaling genomic sequencing technology. We are, however, now at a turning point with the emergence of a whole host of genomic

---

105 Bettinger BT, Wayne DP 2016. Genetic Genealogy in Practice. Arlington, VA: National Genealogical Society.

106 *Dr. Leming Shi, National Center for Toxicological Research.* "MicroArray Quality Control (MAQC) Project". *U.S. Food and Drug Administration.* Retrieved 2007-12-26.

107 *Goetz, Thomas 2017* "23AndMe Will Decode Your DNA for $1,000. Welcome to the Age of Genomics".

108 *Ibid.*

sequencing companies. Beyond 23andMe, however, it's important to highlight the work that has made 23andMe possible, developing competitive and accurate genomic sequencing technology that is commercially available and widely adopted around the world. A few important companies to mention here are Illumina, Thermo-Fisher Scientific, Pacific Biosciences, BGI, Qiagen, and Oxford Nanopore Technology that are paving the way for the genomics future.

CHAPTER 6:

ILLUMINA, CONSUMER GENOMICS, POPULATION GENOMICS, AND THE DRUG DEVELOPMENT FUTURE

———

"Marked by the completion of the Human Genome project, life sciences entered the era of big data."

—CHINA NATIONAL GENEBANK

ILLUMINA DRIVES THE GENE SEQUENCING REVOLUTION

Founded in 1998, Illumina is currently the world's largest genomic sequencing company. They aim to make whole genome sequencing a new standard of care for patient evaluation, diagnosis, and treatment. They want it to be as standard as drawing blood. Their self-identified mission is to "unlock the power of the genome...advancing progress in life sciences and life itself."[109] Operating at the intersection of technology and biology, Illumina builds and sells an impressive lineup of benchtop and production-scale tech that can sequence an organism's genetic material. As of 2014, Illumina's technology was responsible for generating more than 70 percent of the world's sequencing data. Illumina has also made genome sequencing more affordable and accessible for health care providers, companies, and governments around the world. They reduced the cost of genomic sequencing from $48,000 in 2009 to $1,000 in 2014. Illumina's sequencers can now complete forty-eight genome sequences in forty-eight hours.[110]

Illumina, among other companies, has presented us with an entirely new set of questions about what to do with all of this genetic data. Illumina is now working on selling the utility of genomics data as a comprehensive screening tool and standard of care for all patients. Servicing hospitals, research facilities, universities, and pharmaceutical companies, Illumina is behind many of the consumer genomics companies that you may be familiar with, like 23andMe, who provide personal genetic services using the Illumina Infinium® Global Screening Array. This one company has driven the explosion of direct-to-consumer genomics products and services that

109 "Illumina | Sequencing And Array-Based Solutions For Genetic Research." 2020.

110 "Focus: New Machines Can Sequence Human Genome In One Hour, Illumina Announces." 2017. San Diego Union-Tribune.

are working on commercializing and popularizing genomic sequencing for consumer purposes, like tracing ancestry. "It took years and millions of dollars to sequence the human genome," said Maude Champagne, U.S. Marketing Director for Illumina. "Now with companies such as 23andMe, it's something almost everyone can do and access."

Genotyping is the process of determining which genetic variances an individual possesses. Sequencing, on the other hand, is the process of determining the exact sequence of a certain length of DNA.[111] Any given popular genomics direct-to-consumer company uses genotyping, not sequencing to analyze a consumer's DNA, whereas Illumina performs sequencing, not genotyping.[112] The difference is the granularity and level of accuracy of the test performed and the amount of information it may provide. Oftentimes, rather than sequencing a patient's entire genome, they will be sequencing only a portion of DNA, for example, to identify a gene mutation that represents a certain disease. By isolating a portion of genes and conducting this sequencing, a higher degree of accuracy and granularity can be assigned to help researchers look for mutations within targeted and specific genes.[113] Illumina is, however, pushing the boundaries to make whole genome sequencing more cost effective, possible, and comprehensible in the very near term, according to one Illumina employee.

---

111 "Difference Between DNA Genotyping & Sequencing." 2020. 23Andme Customer Care.

112 Ibid.

113 Ibid.

BANKING TO GENOMICS: TYLER BELIEVES IN THE CONSUMER GENOMICS FUTURE

Direct-to-consumer companies like 23andMe and Helix have realized the potential of the genetic blueprint to reveal all sorts of information about ourselves, our history, and where we came from. Helix too has tapped into the consumer side of genomics, which is only just beginning. "What we know about personal genomics now is a fraction of what we are learning every day, and what we will know ten to fifteen years from now," said Tyler Zanini, business developer at Helix.

As a former healthcare investment banker at Credit Suisse, Tyler saw this potential in popular consumer genetics products. He made his move to San Francisco after investment banking in New York City, bridging his background in healthcare and private equity with a deep dive into digital health applications. Tyler saw the emergence of phone and web applications to help patients monitor their chronic conditions and interpreted the market demand for more consumer health information. Thus, Tyler moved to work at Helix where he builds partnerships with companies to help them think about how DNA can apply to their products.

Helix describes itself as a personal genomics company, empowering people to improve their lives through DNA. Helix's motto is "Follow your DNA," and the company offers more than thirty DNA products. Their genetic testing kits include food sensitivity, DNA Fit, Ancestry, Wine Explorer, and the DNA Discovery Kit (to find out your continental ancestry).

Combining genetic data sets with wellness, fitness, nutrition, and lifestyle habits, Helix is trying to offer a platform to consumers to have a new level of precision in shaping their lives, offering consumers factual information about their own bodies. As a consumer, you buy the test online, provide Helix with a sample sent by mail. Then Helix provides the analysis (powered by Illumina's sequencers) and sends you the data as well as access to a web platform to compare your data with others.

Tyler spoke with me about the current dialogue in medical, patient, and consumer communities, driven by the big data movement. According to Tyler, "Genomics should be in the hands of consumers to understand their risk to certain health conditions, and understand how and what to do in their personal lives to address this. As consumers, they can interpret the results, and apply this to their own lives and health."

Genetics, however, aren't deterministic. Instead, they provide insight into our relative risk to certain health conditions. In line with this thinking, Helix offers patients preventative—not diagnostic screening—screening, giving consumers an indication of their relative risk factors, and potentially encouraging them to see health professionals more often or make preventative lifestyle changes.

POPULARIZING GENOMICS DATA

23andMe states their mission is to help people understand and benefit from the human genome. What companies like these are doing is trying to take genetic testing out of the realm of physician's offices. Historically, patients would only undergo a genetic test recommended or prescribed by a physician to identify the probable cause, or link, to a disease. "What we are starting to see across the consumer product landscape, and within medical communities, are gaps in using genetics in patient care," said Tyler.

Again, genetics is a relatively new field. While young physicians are likely to have a broad knowledge base in genetics and understand its applications to patient care, older physicians may not. Remember that the Human Genome Project wasn't completed until 2003, when many current practicing physicians were in training or had already completed medical school. Many physicians, as such, don't have the experience or know how to apply genetics to patient care, or what the new or emerging applications are or may be.

Today, with the emergence of big data, the increasing number of people having genetic testing done, and with our improving abilities to analyze large data sets, we are combining genetic data sets in ways that have never been done before. "This is one of the big challenges," said Tyler. "Of the 7.5 billion people living on earth today, only about ten to fifteen million have undergone a genetic test."

Another challenge is the fragmented databases housing this information. Some scientific communities are beginning to come together to link databases and genetic information and research. But as long as these communities remain divided, we cannot share data and our ability to link and identify patterns in genetic sequencing remains impaired. How do we get more people to have genetic testing done and get these tests into the hands of people around the world? Illumina, for one, has initiated partnerships with national governments to support population genomics programs, large shared databases housed in countries that can generate more insights, and realizes the value in these insights.

GOVERNMENT PARTNERSHIPS AND REGULATION ARE ESSENTIAL FOR GENOMICS SUCCESS

23andMe has attracted millions in investments from Google, Genentech, New Enterprise Associates, and Mohr Davidow Ventures. They've also attracted attention from regulators.

In 2010, the company received notice from the FDA that their genetic tests sold to consumers were technically classified as medical devices and would need to be approved by the FDA if commercial licensing were to continue. A similar notice was sent to Illumina, who makes the chips and instruments used by 23andMe in providing its service. [114]

A lapse in communication between the FDA and 23andMe led to an order from the FDA to stop the production and manufacturing of their saliva DNA kits and Personal Genome Services. This is still very new and uncharted territory for the FDA and for the medical device community. This relationship has laid the initial groundwork for what other companies will do in the future with the FDA, as well as sending a message to the public about the safety,

---

114 "Alpha-1 Antitrypsin Deficiency." 2020. En.Wikipedia.org.

efficacy, and accuracy of the products companies are producing and consumers are consuming. While the bulk of products offered by 23andMe now legally saleable in the U.S. are strictly ancestor related, they continue to offer health-related products and services for commercial sale in Canada and the U.K.[115]

However, the FDA has since approved applications for ten genetic tests for 23andMe, including Alzheimer's, Parkinson's, cardiac disease, hereditary thrombophilia, alpha-1 antitrypsin deficiency, glucose-6-phosphate dehydrogenase deficiency, early onset of dystonia, Factor XI deficiency, and Gaucher's disease.[116]

ILLUMINA SUPPORTS POPULATION GENOMICS PROGRAMS

Illumina, in their meticulously planned long-term strategy, recognizes that their market success must be paralleled with an equally effective non-market strategy. Illumina is working to sell governments on the utility of genomics data to improve their health care systems, supporting many international Precision Medicine initiatives with their sequencers. They've also supported national population genomics programs to develop a large national database of genomic data, of particular value in the ability to compare these data sets. Here are examples of population genomics programs:

---

115 Ibid.
116 "Gaucher's Disease." 2020. En.Wikipedia.org.

ILLUMINA SUPPORTED NATIONAL POPULATION GENOMICS PROGRAMS

Australia: Australia has several population genomics programs, including Australian Genomics Health Alliance and Genomics Health Futures Mission. These were established to apply genomics to healthcare and unite healthcare intuitions.

France: Some of France's population genomics programs include the French National Alliance for Life Sciences and Health and the French Genomics Medicine Plan 2025. They are tasked with determining how to use genomics sequencing in healthcare and establishing a National Genomics Medicine Framework and sequence 235,000 genomes by 2020.

Saudi Arabia: Saudi Arabia's genomics initiatives are managed by the King Abdulaziz City for Science and Technology and the Saudi Human Genome Program, which aim to sequence 100,000 genomes for early treatment of disease and preventative treatment.

Turkey: Turkey's Health Institute and Turkish Genome Project are working to sequence 100,000 human genomes from healthy individuals and individuals with rare and complex diseases, and to establish a National BioBank infrastructure.

China: China's population genomics initiatives are numerous, but include the work of intuitions such as the China National Genebank, the Chinese Academy of Sciences, and China's Precision Medicine Initiative. In 2017, the China National Genebank set out to sequence 100,000 human genomes of Chinese citizens by 2020. The Chinese Academy of Sciences indicated plans to use the genetic data of the Han ethnic majority and nine other ethnic minority groups to decode hereditary information within genes and gather genetic information. China's Precision Medicine Initiative aims to sequence 10 million human genomes by 2030.

Denmark: Denmark has launched Genome Denmark and National Genome Center to establish a country level platform for sequencing and bioinformatics for universities, hospitals, and private companies, and the creation of a "Danish Reference Genome."

USA: The U.S. genomics initiatives are also numerous such as the National Human Genome Research Institute, Project Baseline, Amazon Genomics, All of Us, Microsoft Genomics, and IBM Watson for Genomics. Some of the goals include determining how much of the genome contributes to health, and how much is influenced by lifestyle, and applying AI to generate insights and pattern recognition to genomics data.

UK: The U.K. also has multiple genomics initiatives, including Genomics England, Scottish and Welsh Genomics for Precision Medicine, Northern Ireland Genomics Medicine Center. These initiatives were setup to deliver 100,000 Genome Project, sequence patients with rare diseases and cancers and family members, and are part of a national precision medicine strategy. The sequencing goal is to sequence 100,000 genomes by 2018.

Brazil: Part of the Brazil Initiative on precision Medicine aims to support Brazil's genomic databases and National Precision Medicine Initiative.

Switzerland: The Swiss Personalized Network is the creation of a nationally coordinated data infrastructure to enable interoperability with an emphasis on clinical data management systems. Beyond that, the vision is to integrate public health and healthy citizen data.

Japan: Japan's Genomic Medicine Program supports an integrated database of genomic medicine from initiatives like Biobank Japan, and Tohoku Medical Megabank.

Qatar: Qatar's Genome project supports genomics initiatives with a direct clinical impact, targeting national priority diseases such as diabetes and cardiovascular disorders.

Finland: Part of Finland's National Genome Strategy is ensuring that genomic data will be used effectively to help improve human health and well-being.

Netherlands: RADICON NL is researching the added value of whole genome sequencing as a first-tier test in the care of those with a rare genetic disease.

Estonia: Estonia's Genome Project is a population-based biological database and biobank.

This illustrates how globally widespread the interest in genomics has become in using it as a tool to improve healthcare systems and patient outcomes. The value of having national population genomics programs is having large aggregate data sets from which to compare and draw insights using machine learning and artificial intelligence. However, genomics data sharing at a national level stops where country boundaries begin. Many countries, while using Illumina's sequencers and developing such national genomics programs, are unwilling to share genomics data internationally. Illumina describes itself as a hardware company—primarily selling instruments and related materials—rather than a data management company. Illumina stores its genomics data after sequencing on Amazon's AWS cloud. Moreover, Illumina does not have access or rights to patients' genomics data. In January 2020, however, Illumina announced at the JP Morgan Healthcare Conference the rolling out of new software and analytics platforms to help users better decipher genomics data.[117] With the decline in sequencing costs and the bulk of Illumina's revenue coming from materials to run sequencers, they may need to adjust their business model to offer greater insights into the sequencing data they are generating.

WITH MORE INSIGHT, GENOMICS DATA COULD BE THE NEW OIL
I interviewed Shu Tao, a PhD bioinformaticist at City of Hope Hospital in California. He is a scientist who reads and interprets genomics data sets for cancer patients. The purpose of his work is to determine what all this information means in the context of a cancer patient's health or determine what degree of probability a patient may develop a certain type of cancer. Shu's work can be tedious, reading through and trying to understand these data sets. "My team is beginning to apply algorithms and analytics tools to help understand and decipher the data to make it manageable," he said. "Specifically, algorithms are designed based on patterns identified in large genetic data sets which are then translated to computer

---

117 "Illumina Announces New Sequencing System, Partnership With Roche And Software Suite To Accelerate Adoption Of Genomics." 2020. Benzinga.

models to help clients interpret how genetic variation affects crucial cellular processes. For example, it may show us how disruption to the normal functioning of these pathways can potentially cause diseases such as cancer."

ILLUMINA'S ANALYTICS TOOLS

Illumina acknowledges it will need to adjust its business model to help professionals like Shu interpret genomics data, but these are still limited. "We understand about 1 percent of human genetic makeup, and what different genes are responsible for, and how they operate both collectively and individually," said geneticist Victor Li. We not only have to develop new tools and software to manage and understand this data, but we also have to retrain healthcare professionals and physicians for it to have greater patient utility. Illumina realizes this and has initiated a partnership with Apple, among others, to create the MyGenome app for visualizing genomic data. They're also launching their NextSeq 1000 2000 with Dragen data analysis to generate greater insights from highly accurate genetic reads and tests.

CLINICAL APPLICATIONS OF GENOMICS DATA

Three main segments of clinical activities for Illumina being used today are:

1. **Comprehensive genomic profiling for cancer:** Using genomic profiling in cancer patients, physicians can identify the gene variants triggering cancer and hypothesize how patients may react to certain treatments. It can also be used to determine a genetic predisposition for certain

cancers, which can help in earlier detection, treatment, and better outcomes.

2. **Identification of rare, undiagnosed diseases:** There are many diseases today that aren't well understood, which may have a basis in genetics. Having a better and more complete understanding of the human genome and how it works can help us better understand and study diseases we don't understand, and even how to treat them, like my own disease, Stargardt's.

3. **Prenatal screening** Prenatal screening can be used to determine the chances of a fetus having certain disorders like Down syndrome. [118]

Our knowledge and ability to apply genetics to clinical treatment and testing in applications such as these will only continue to grow as more patients have their genomes sequenced and as we generate more insights from this data.

GENOMICS AS A TOOL FOR DRUG DEVELOPMENT

One side of genetics is tailored to identifying patient treatments, drugs, and identifying metabolic pathways specific to patients. This side of genetics is based in medical care. Beyond giving the doctor a more holistic sense of how you should be treated, genomic sequencing could also have implications for the FDA when reviewing and approving new drugs. "Sequencing may alter or even revolutionize how drugs are developed, reviewed, and approved, even streamlining the process," said Maude Champagne, whom

---

118 "NIPT Non-Invasive Prenatal Testing | Integrated Genetics." 2020. Integratedgenetics.com.

I interviewed. Maude works as the U.S. marketing director at Illumina.

Imagine that a patient group with a disease is identified through sequencing for a company that is developing a disease treatment. Rather than launching a random clinical trial that gives the drug to a study group of patients that may or may not have the disease, you could instead identify this group of patients ahead of time. You could also design the drug in its earliest development stages around the genetic sequence or mutation of the patient group, hence the interest in transitioning from "pharmaceutical" to "biopharmaceutical."

What is exciting and incredible is that this is already happening. As a patient with Stargardt's, there are several ongoing clinical trials I've been contacted about. Genomics data has become a precious commodity, and global pharmaceutical giants are investing. GlaxoSmithKline invested $300 million in 23andMe to identify new R&D targets to fill clinical trials. In 2015, Genentech and Pfizer both structured deals that permitted access to data from 800,000 genotyped individuals. "The more data that pharma can tap into through tests like the ones developed by Foundation Medicine or 23andMe, and through partnerships with data companies, the more shots on goal we'll have to discover the truly breakthrough therapies," says Jon Roffman, a managing principal in ZS Associates' oncology business.[119]

---

119 Editors, ZS. 2020. "DNA-Based Data Is A Hot Commodity, And Pharma Is Buying." Info.Zs.com.

This data purchasing and partnership trend can be seen in other recent partnerships as well, such as Roche's acquisition of Flatiron Health and Foundation Medicine, AstraZeneca's collaboration with Microsoft and Human Longevity, Illumina's sponsorship of population genomics programs, Regeneron's partnerships with the UK Biobank and Geisinger Health, and Amgen's purchase of deCODE Genetics.[120] A common application that may apply to a large patient group is Pfizer's partnership with 23andMe to identify genes associated with depression to better understand its genetic drivers and how to treat it.[121] And Illumina is working on partnerships with insurers to work toward covering the cost of genetic sequencing with Cigna, for example.[122]

These partnerships are already transitioning from research into clinical trials, with new drugs in GSK's work with 23andMe on Parkinson's, which aims to target a specific mutation associated with the disease. 23andMe has identified 250 patients with the corresponding genetic profile for the clinical trial when they are ready to begin testing. For cancer patients, Illumina partnered with Bristol Myers Squibb to tailor cancer treatments already on the market, OPDIVO® and Yervoy, to specific patients to ensure more effective outcomes.

If we can generate insights as quickly as we can sequence an individual's data, genomics data could become invaluable

---

120 Editors, ZS. 2020. "DNA-Based Data Is A Hot Commodity, And Pharma Is Buying." Info.Zs.com.

121 "Using Crowd-Sourced Data To Find Genetic Links To Depression | Pfizer." 2020. Pfizer.com.

122 "Cigna Issues Coverage Criteria For Whole-Exome Sequencing; WGS Still Not Covered." 2020. Genomeweb.

and is already increasing in value. The race in the twenty-first century will be to understand what all of this genomics data means and how it can be clinically applied.

PROGRESS IN SEQUENCING CONTINUES

Imagine that Illumina's vision is realized, and genomic sequencing becomes a new standard of evaluating patients at any medical facility for any medical issue. Imagine that it takes ten minutes to have your genome sequenced with a meaningful analysis for the physician to review. Rather than filling out medical charts in the waiting room to then be asked additional questions by the nurse and doctor, you have your genome sequenced and all this information is automatically provided. Imagine that the doctor's course of treatment is referring to your genomic sequence as a baseline. All the medicines he prescribes and procedures he performs are based on this. This means dietary recommendations could be more precise, and warning signs for genetic susceptibility for cancer or heart disease could be realized sooner and treated accordingly. It would mean that rather than asking if you have any known allergies for medications and prescribing a few to see which works, the physician could automatically match your genetic sequence with the most effective medication on the market.

Oxford Nanopore Technologies is one company to watch in the genomic sequencing space and may be paving the way for new sequencing technology using nanotechnology. They have been developing the first portable genome sequencer to lower costs without sacrificing accuracy. Think of the revolution portable computers had on the global economy and on our work. Now think what this could mean in the context of sequencing. A farmer may do crop sequencing on his iPhone one day and use an analytics tool to interpret and understand what it means for how he should breed crops in preparation for optimal crop yields in the future.

CHAPTER 7:

CRISPR CAS9: GENE EDITING'S NEW PLATFORM FOR PRECISION MEDICINE

——

"The first monkeys were born with genomes that had been rewritten through precision gene editing, bringing the steady march of CRISPR research right to Homo sapiens' evolutionary front door."

– JENNIFER A. DOUDNA[123]

---

123 Doudna, Jennifer. 2017. A Crack in Creation: Gene Editing and the Unthinkable Power to Control Evolution

GENE EDITING TOOLS: ORIGINS

The idea of editing genes isn't a new one. Doing it efficiently, precisely, and on a level that can be scaled, however, is. 2012 marked a new breakthrough for genetics with the discovery of CRISPR-Cas9 gene-editing technology. Microsoft hails CRISPR-Cas9 as part of the living software revolution, which many anticipate as being one of the next greatest human paradigm shifts. To appreciate how far we've come and how this pace has accelerated recently, what this breakthrough means, and where we're going in the future with genetics and gene editing, it's important to consider the groundwork that has been laid with prior gene-editing discoveries. Building the cumulative knowledge of scientific curiosity, discovery, and determination has led us to where we are today, with CRISPR-Cas9.

- **DNA Ligases** – In 1967, DNA ligases were discovered; these are responsible for the repair and replication of DNA in all organisms. Phosphodiester bonds allow DNA strands to join together. This discovery helped lay the groundwork for other experiments that spliced DNA in the 1960s and 1970s.[124]

---

124 "Hepatitis B." 2019. Who.Int.

- **Restriction Enzymes** – Then in 1968, restriction enzymes were discovered along with "molecular scissors" that could identify and cut foreign DNA. In 1972, researchers developed the first recombinant DNA, or DNA created from the elements of two different organisms. This work showed that it was possible for any two DNA molecules to be joined together. It was also realized that recombinant DNA will replicate naturally, despite its artificial combination with or introduction to another organism's DNA.

- **Genentech and the Synthetic Insulin Breakthrough** – In the 1980s, a number of genetic experiments emerged that had tangible use. Genentech brought the first genetically engineered drug—synthetic insulin—to market in 1982. Insulin harvested from animals had been on the market for patients with Type 1 diabetes but was expensive and inefficient. In 1978, one pound of insulin required 8,000 pancreas glands and 23,500 animals for production. The demand for insulin outpaced our ability to produce it using the animal harvesting method.[125] Synthetic insulin production was a tremendous breakthrough for genetic engineering that had a direct application to improving human health.

- **Polymerase Chain Reaction** – In 1983, the polymerase chain reaction (PCR) was discovered, which enabled researchers to make many copies of a specific DNA segment. Through the chain reaction, a copy of a DNA segment can be replicated thousands or even millions of times to produce many commercial products. This significantly cut down on the time it took to "clone" DNA. From this discovery, scientists realized our ability to

---

125 "Synthego | Full Stack Genome Engineering." 2020. Synthego.com.

isolate a desired piece of DNA and grow it in colonies of bacteria tenfold. Scientists now had the ability to "mass produce" genes, but it still took significant time to identify the desired gene. This changed in 1985, when Zinc Finger Nuclease was discovered, which enabled us to "recognize" DNA, or a specific gene, and cleave or cut it, as it could bind to three specific base DNA pairs and can be continued to recognize longer sequences.[126]

- **Recombinant DNA Vaccines** – In 1986, the first recombinant DNA vaccine was approved by the FDA for treating Hepatitis B. This method for vaccine development became the standard for many vaccines, including ones that dealt with HPV, whooping cough, and shingles.

- **GMOs** – In 1988, the first GMO crop was developed, Bt-corn, which could increase crop yields by detracting pests through its gene edit, or genetic recombination. This resulted in a new wave of GMO crops globally to maximize food production.[127]

- **Human Genome Project** – From 1990–2003, the Human Genome Project mapped the entire human genome for the first time, identifying more than 20,000 genes and their genomic loci. In 1999, scientists working on the project completely mapped out the sequence for chromosome 22.

- **Elements of CRISPR** – In 1993, the initial elements of CRISPR were discovered.

- **Cloning** – In 1996, Dolly the sheep was successfully cloned, and in 2003, the first cloning of an endangered animal was done.

---

126 "Hepatitis B." 2019. Who.Int.
127 Ibid.

- **Gene Therapy** – In 2001, the first gene-targeted drug therapy was approved by the FDA as an anti-cancer drug for chronic myelogenous leukemia, which is still used today. This has influenced a wave of targeted gene therapy cancer drugs, and many pharmaceutical firms globally today are building up their immune-oncology pipeline with these approaches. 2010 showed us a new release of several lines of FDA approved gene therapies for several diseases.[128]
- **ENCODE** – In 2003, after the completion of the first entire mapping of the human genome, the ENCODE (Encyclopedia of DNA Elements) project was launched, with the objective to develop a complete list of the functional elements of the human genome.
- **Crop Endorsement** – In 2004, the United Nations formally endorsed biotech crops as a way of supporting struggling farmers in developing nations to try solving the world's hunger crisis. [129]
- **Cancer Treatments** – In 2006, Gardasil, which used gene-editing, became the first preventative cancer treatment on the market, the commonly known HPV vaccine for women. [130]
- **Stem Cell Programming** – In 2006, Dr. Shinya Yamanaka introduced induced pluripotent stem cell (iPSC) technology. His team isolated fibroblasts (first from mice, later from humans) and reprogrammed them into stem cell state via expression of a mix of four genetic factors. These

128 "Hepatitis B." 2019. Who.Int.
129 "Biotech Foods Endorsed By U.N. Agency." 2004. Msnbc.com.
130 Ibid.

iPSCs could then differentiate into any specific cell type that the researchers wished to investigate. [131]

- **Synthetic Life Forms** – Then, in 2011, a scientist created the world's first synthetic life form. This technically meant a living organism was entirely built, rather than evolved or born. In this experiment, a 1.08-mega-base pair *Mycoplasma mycoides* JCVI-syn1.0 genome was created by Craig Venter and his team and transplanted into an *M. capricolum* recipient cell to create the new *M. mycoides* cells controlled entirely by the synthetic chromosome. This was important because it proved that life could be created synthetically, which has a multitude of applications in genetics.

- **CRISPR-Cas9** – In 2012, CRISPR –Cas9 is discovered, marking a new era in gene-editing possibilities.

SETTING THE STAGE FOR THE LIVING SOFTWARE REVOLUTION

While gene editing has been a theoretical idea to treat disease for over fifty years, the recent discovery of CRISPR-Cas9 is making this a reality. CRISPR stands for clustered regularly interspaced short philanthropic repeats. In 2015, while working together in a lab at UC Berkeley, Jennifer Doudna and Emmanuelle Charpentier invented this new technology for editing genomes. The advantage of their new technology is that it is not only a more efficient gene-editing mechanism, but it is also more precise than any other gene-editing tools we've had before.[132] "We realized we could harness this func-

---

131 S, Takahashi. 2020. "Induction Of Pluripotent Stem Cells From Mouse Embryonic And Adult Fibroblast Cultures By Defined Factors. – PubMed – NCBI." Ncbi.Nlm.Nih.gov.

132 Doudna, Jennifer. 2020. "How CRISPR Lets Us Edit Our DNA." Ted.com.

tion as a genetic engineering technology—a way for scientists to delete or insert specific bits of DNA into cells with incredible precision," said Doudna.[133]

Before CRISPR's discovery, gene editing was a slower, more cumbersome process. Think of CRISPR-Cas9 as a "system" that can directly cleave DNA threads and insert the new gene or genes, rather than using enzymes to cut the DNA and a separate tool or mechanism to insert the new gene. In addition to cutting the DNA thread and inserting a new gene in one "system," CRISPR can edit several genes simultaneously—another major breakthrough.[134]

CRISPR-Cas9 is proving to be an alternative that is more efficient and one that we can customize to other existing genome editing tools. Since the CRISPR-Cas9 system itself is capable of cutting DNA strands, CRISPRs do not need to be paired with separate cleaving enzymes as other tools do. They can also easily be matched with tailor-made "guide" RNA (gRNA) sequences designed to lead them to their DNA targets. Tens of thousands of such gRNA sequences have already been created and are available to the research community.[135]

So, what are the implications of an efficient and precise gene-editing system? Linking this gene-editing platform can help edit a disease causing gene mutation. It can be a new way of developing drugs, creating new agricultural crops, and helping with the treatment of diseases through gene modification.

---

133 Ibid.
134 "Questions And Answers About CRISPR." 2014. Broad Institute.
135 Doudna, Jennifer. 2020. "How CRISPR Lets Us Edit Our DNA." Ted.com.

We are just beginning to consider CRISPR's many possibilities and the potential implications of this technology. For one, our understanding of the genome and the implications of what genes mean and all of the different structures that build off of the blueprint are still very limited. We don't yet know the implications of some types of gene editing.

Nessan Bermingham is a former Chief Executive Officer at Intellia Therapeutics, one of the three CRISPR companies that went public in 2016. According to one source, Nessan said, "People have been talking about (personalized medicine) for twenty years and yet we've never had a system to allow us to do it before. And for the first time ever, we actually have a system to do it and that system would be based on your personalized genome." [136] The implications of this technology are thrilling, fascinating, and also frightening. But as advances continue to be made, it's important for us to all understand their implications for our own health and for the good of society.

As we learn more about the genome, we've become better at genetic engineering and gained more understanding about what characteristics the expression of certain genes will show. We have become more precise and efficient—and with AI and cloud computing technology and the ability to rapidly sequence genomic data—we can apply these principles to CRISPR-Cas9 to solve problems from increasing crop yields to treating human diseases to developing alternative energy sources to fossil fuels.

---

136 McKinsey and Company. "Realizing the Potential of CRISPR." January 2017.

ETHICAL QUESTIONS AND GENE EDITING

While we may think of genomic engineering as a brand-new science, we've been using principles of genetic engineering for centuries with the development of modern agriculture. Selecting the genes from one crop over another for more favorable growing conditions, for bigger cows that produce more milk, for example, we recognized the principles of favorable gene expression before ever cutting and pasting DNA strands together in a lab.

At the current rate of discovery and advances in genetics, I can see a future in which we "edit" the genes of living patients to cure them of their genetic disease. I sometimes think about this in relation to the gene mutation that causes my progressive vision loss. In what ways has this condition impacted my thinking, my emotions, my relationships, and my own experience of being human? Would "fixing" this gene fundamentally change my identity and my human experience? Maybe for the better. But by taking this technology a few steps further, could we apply the same principle to mental illness, manic depression, and other conditions that cause challenges in a patient's life, but are also intertwined in their personality and identity? Taken in certain directions, genetically engineering who we are could have unsavory implications for everyone. This new paradigm will force us to fundamentally consider what it means to be human. Are we only our genes? To what extent does the environment play a role in who we are and how does our genetic material work as an expression of selfhood?

Consider selective breeding with horses to make those used in racing faster, stronger, or more beautiful. Or consider breeding dogs to keep the offspring "pure." And think to your own preferences in choosing a spouse—is some of this based in biology and influenced by an underlying desire to create viable offspring that will be healthy, intelligent, strong, and likely to survive in our modern world?

CRISPR'S MECHANICS HARNESS THE POWER OF NATURE

Something I find inspirational about CRISPR-Cas9 as a tool to harness the power of gene editing is that it isn't man-made—it is instead harnessing the power of a naturally occurring process and tool in nature.[137] Rather than inventing our own means of editing genes, we are influencing one of nature's own stratagems.

Doudna and Charpentier's discovery began with an experiment studying bacteria to understand how they combated viral infections. CRISPR developed naturally as an evolutionary survival mechanism to protect bacteria and provide immunity against viral infections. When viruses enter into a cell, they inject their DNA into the cell. The CRISPR system in bacterium allows that DNA to be plucked out of the virus and inserted into little bits into the chromosome and the DNA of the bacterium so it can "recognize" the virus and develop "immunity" form the viral infection when re-exposed. These integrated bits of viral DNA get inserted at a site called CRISPR. This insertion, in turn, fundamentally

---

137 Zhang, Feng. 2015. "CRISPR/Cas9: Prospects And Challenges." Human Gene Therapy 26 (7): 409-410.

alters the DNA sequence of that bacterium from its original sequence.

"We can think of these viral infestations in bacteria as ticking time bombs—the bacteria only have moments to defuse the bomb before they are destroyed," said Jennifer Doudna.[138] Some bacteria have developed an evolutionary mechanism to quickly detect and destroy the viral DNA. These immune systems are termed CRISPR, which allows the bacteria to detect and destroy the viral DNA. Part of this immune system is a protein—Cas9—which is able to detect, cut, and eventually degrade the viral DNA. CRISPR enables the cell to memorize over time the viruses it has been exposed to, ultimately acquiring immunity. Most importantly, this memory in the DNA is passed down when the bacterium divides and reproduces, so the offspring inherits the immunity, increasing the chances of survival and the bacterium's evolutionary success. So, over many generations, cells are protected against infections with these genetic sequences.

Once these bits of DNA have been inserted back into the bacterial chromosome, the cell makes a copy of the viral RNA. This RNA is an exact replicate of the viral DNA. RNA is a "chemical cousin" of DNA. With a matching sequence between DNA and RNA, the two can interact. So, these identical bits of DNA and RNA bind to the Cas9 protein and form a complex. This complex then searches through all of the DNA in the cell and the RNA. When it matches two identical sequences in each, it matches them together, and

---

138 Doudna, Jennifer. 2020. "How CRISPR Lets Us Edit Our DNA." Ted.com.

precisely cleaves or cuts the viral DNA. Thus, the Cas9 RNA is like a pair of scissors cutting a DNA strand. [139]

This CRISPR-Cas9 discovery is being applied to many situations beyond a bacterium's immune response to destroying a viral invader and acquiring immunity. It can also be applied to editing the human genome itself, replacing one gene with another. Think of editing a brown-eyed gene for a blue-eyed one. The possible applications, however, go far beyond these examples.

CRISPR APPLICATIONS AND THE FUTURE OF GENE EDITING

One application of CRISPR technology, beyond editing genes, is using it to directly test for casual genetic variations related to human disease.[140] Because CRISPR can quickly match DNA that it has encountered before, by matching its "memory," a new piece of DNA for which it has no match can show us genetic variations different from a typical gene sequence, or a certain code with a certain gene. A difference from this code would have no match. By quickly scanning through all of the genes in the genome, new gene candidates—from a variety of assays ranging from cancer drug resistance to neurodegeneration—will inform new strategies for combating diseases.[141]

139 Doudna, Jennifer. 2020. "How CRISPR Lets Us Edit Our DNA." Ted.com.
140 Zhang, Feng. 2015. "CRISPR/Cas9: Prospects And Challenges." Human Gene Therapy 26 (7): 409-410.
141 Ibid.

Charpentier realized that beyond bacterium, CRISPR-Cas9 could be applied as a platform for genetic engineering. Using Cas9, they could delete or insert specific bits of DNA into cells in a more precise and efficient way, opening up a whole new range of possibilities. What is important to note here, and what Doudna and Charpentier realized, is that this complex is programmable. It can be programmed to recognize particular DNA sequences and then cut and insert other DNA strands.[142]

Think of using a word processing program to fix a typo in a document. Our cells have an ability to detect errors, or typos, in their own sequencing and repair them. They can paste together broken ends of DNA with a small change in the sequence of the gene position or by integrating a new piece of DNA at the site of the cut.

As such, cells can be triggered to edit a gene sequence by either the disruption or incorporation of new genetic material. So, returning to our apple example, let's say we want to make apples that are sweeter and crispier. This is a technology we could apply to editing the apple tree's genome to produce the desired apple.

So, in theory, if CRISPR can be programmed to identify a mutation in a gene sequence causing Stargardt's disease, we could trigger cells to repair the mutation causing the disease.

CRISPR technology has already had a number of direct applications. Today it is being used for developing cancer

---

142 Ibid.

treatments, fighting obesity, and creating hornless cows. In 2018, the first CRISPR human clinical trial was approved by Vertex Pharmaceuticals and CRISPR Therapeutics for the blood disorder B-thalassemia.[143] If the treatment is successful, it could be the end of this disorder and sickle cell anemia. Think about not just treating the symptoms of the disease, but directly treating the source through genetics. For example, my own eye disease causes gradual vision loss because of a genetic mutation of a gene that processes Vitamin A. CRISPR's application to my own disease could be to edit this gene mutation, replacing it with a normal one. In theory, Vitamin A would then be properly processed, stopping the gradual vision loss.

THE NEXT STEPS: LOOKING AT GENES COLLECTIVELY AND GENE DRIVES

It isn't quite as simple as editing a single mutated gene to "cure" a disease. We now think of genes as operating together and collectively, rather than individually. DNA recombinant technology and its applications have helped revolutionize our understanding of what certain genes do functionally, and also how they may work together collectively.

Though CRISPR was seen for its revolutionary potential in disease treatment, Kevin Esvelt took the idea to a whole new level when he realized the potential of CRISPR gene drives. Gene drives are genetic elements that "cheat evolution" by biasing their transmission to offspring beyond Mendelian

---

143 Zhang, Feng. 2015. "CRISPR/Cas9: Prospects And Challenges." Human Gene Therapy 26 (7): 409-410.

laws. CRISPR-based gene drives may have promising potential in eradicating malaria and other vector-borne diseases.[144]

SUMMARY

The early promise of genetic engineering in the 1970s was slowed by its inefficient techniques that were too difficult for widespread use or for application in clinical trials on a level that could be scaled commercially. We had to use several tools—enzymes, for example—to edit genomes, often with many mistakes. This was before the Human Genome Project, and our understanding of how genes worked to express certain traits was significantly limited compared to today (though our understanding is still quite limited).

Scaling this technology is still something companies are struggling to finance. While we've discovered CRISPR-Cas9 and use it in many research experiments, we're still working to understand how DNA edits and repairs itself after cuts. We are still only in the initial stages of understanding how the genome works, let alone understanding how editing it causes other genes before and after it to be expressed or not.

Despite its expense as a challenge, in the business world of biotechnology and pharmaceuticals, CRISPR has spurred an emergence of new specialties, positions, and fields of research. We need to invest in these advances to continue our progress.

These breakthroughs in editing the genome more precisely and efficiently and the ability to quickly and cost-effectively

---

144 "Synthego | Full Stack Genome Engineering." 2020. Synthego.com.

sequence the genome leave us with an entirely new set of possibilities. These extend beyond implications for human health and agriculture to other possibilities we cannot yet imagine. It has also led to the creation of an entirely new set of companies and approaches to gene editing. We are only at the beginning. If you're interested in staying up to date on the latest CRISPR developments, check out the web platform in the following footnote—it links to more than sixty podcasts and various news sources on CRISPR.[145]

145 "Synthego | Full Stack Genome Engineering." 2020. Synthego.com.

CHAPTER 8:

CRISPR COMPANIES AND COMPUTATIONAL BIOLOGY

"The most remarkable feature of life is that it is both a process that reads and expresses a program, and a process that builds the machine that does that."

—*ANTOINE DANCHIN*[146]

CRISPR'S NEW ERA OF SCIENTIFIC PIONEERS

The simplicity and specificity with which CRISPR-Cas9 can edit DNA is changing the pace of biological research. CRISPR is helping drive precision medicine forward in identifying and understanding mechanisms of genetic diseases, validating disease targets, developing animal disease models, facilitating genetic engineering in plants, and allowing for

---

146 Danchin, Antoine. *The Delphic Boat*. Harvard University Press. 2002.

more thorough epigenetic gene therapy. Combined with breakthroughs in cost-effective, efficient genome sequencing, we have now identified over three thousand genes associated with disease-causing mutations.

CRISPR-Cas9 as a technology is driving a whole new set of skills and ways of thinking about biology. Historically, chemistry and biology were two separate disciplines before being combined into biochemistry. We are seeing the same wave with the rise of computer science, genetics, and biology—now commonly termed computational biology—which is being applied to CRISPR experiments.

Bradley Murray is a biology graduate I interviewed from Georgetown University. He is a researcher and pioneer working to drive innovation, discovery, and business in the CRISPR genomics world. With an undergraduate degree in biology as his only formal scientific academic training, Bradley is among a new generation of scientific pioneers not focused purely on academic research but on commercial applications of CRISPR technology. He realized a traditional PhD route wasn't one he wanted to pursue, nor would it keep pace with the rate of discovery and application of CRISPR technology and the frontier of the emerging field of computational biology. Bradley's logic is this: "If you spend a few years in a lab understanding the fundamentals of how this research is being conducted, are intelligent, can learn quickly, and have good computer skills, you don't need a PhD to do what I do."

Bradley works as a computational biologist. He has spent two-and-a-half years working in cancer genomics, researching genetic variations that cause tumor growth and identifying variations that do and don't respond to treatments. He's done genome discovery work to identify genetic causes of disease. He made the move to one of only three existing CRISPR companies in the U.S.—Intellia Therapeutics.

A MULTILINGUIST

Bradley likes to think of his profession as a multilinguist. As a biologist, he is able to speak and understand the language of genetics. As a computer scientist and programmer, he is able to apply computer programming and computer languages to genetics. As one of the few young multi-linguists in the rapidly emerging field of computational biology, Bradley is able to speak deeply to aspects of the industry that will define future medicine.

Outside of Bradley's work as a computational biologist, he is earning a Master's in Business Administration to add to his skill set and to build a better business in the biotechnology world. "Early stage innovative medicines with data focus are the skills and industry I know—I want to build biotech with this skill set," said Bradley.

Bradley's average workday involves about a third of his time spent writing code, another third doing exploratory data analysis, and the last third talking to people to collaborate and solve problems. Bradley ensures that CRISPR gene edits made in cell cultures are efficient and that the cuts are made in the correct areas that are identified and predetermined in a computer model.

Bradley thinks the potential gene-editing power of CRISPR implies a future where we could treat heritable genetic diseases with gene edits. His company works on gene edits in the liver, a soft tissue that is suspected to show early success, and diseases of the liver are currently well understood. Bradley is working with a team that is developing software to use with CRISPR gene editing, which includes making predictions and measurements and validating these measurements in gene edits—it isn't just about writing a new code or a new genetic sequence. With every new gene sequence, there is a tremendous amount of detailed work and analysis that follows. Once a new gene sequence has been designed in the software program, the sequences can be synthesized in a lab, put into cells and animals, and designed in silicon before going in vitro or in vivo. In vitro experiments are performed with cells or microorganisms outside of their normal biological context. Think of these as test-tube experiments or experimenting with cell cultures in Petri dishes. In vivo experiments, by contrast, are conducted within whole living organisms, like in humans or plants.

PRECISION MEDICINE APPLICATIONS

In Bradley's mind, Hemoglobinopathies and CAR T-cell therapy are two of the most immediate applications of his research. In these cases, you don't have to address the delivery challenge of gene editing. The focus then turns to the most difficult barrier to potential in vivo use of CRISPR-Cas9, delivery.[147]

---

147 Lino, Christopher A., Jason C. Harper, James P. Carney, and Jerilyn A. Timlin. 2018. "Delivering CRISPR: A Review Of The Challenges And Approaches." Drug Delivery 25 (1): 1234-1257.

In order to optimize therapeutic potential, the appropriate delivery, specificity, and repair strategies must be established.[148] While the field of computational biology is moving quickly and research is being conducted around the world, there is a laundry list of unknowns that need to be addressed, such as *how* genes should be edited or *if* they should be edited at all.

ESTABLISHING STANDARDS FOR GENE EDITING

The National Institution of Standards and Technology (NIST) is meeting to determine what some of these gene-editing implications may be.[149] Bradley sits on the NIST Gene Editing Committee, where a scientific panel is putting together standards for gene editing. Some of these standards include how you make a gene edit and how you measure it.

CRISPR COMPANY DEVELOPMENTS—A NOT SO SCIENCE FICTION FUTURE

While CRISPR gene-editing technology may sound like a distant, science fiction future, we are experimenting today in human trials to test its effectiveness and begin to understand how patient treatments unfold. "Just three years ago we were talking about CRISPR-based treatments as a sci-fi

---

148 Zhang, Feng. 2015. "CRISPR/Cas9: Prospects And Challenges." Human Gene Therapy 26 (7): 409-410.

149 "NIST Genome Editing Consortium." 2020. National Institute of Standards and Technology.

fantasy," CRISPR Therapeutics CEO Samarth Kulkarni said. "But here we are."[150]

One of the most well-known early gene therapy trials involved two studies from France and the U.K. of children suffering from X-linked severe combined immunodeficiency (SCID X-1).[151] Of the twenty patients participating in the trial, seventeen were successfully and stably cured.[152] However, five children subsequently developed T-cell leukemia, with one child dying from chemotherapy-refractory leukemia.

Early efforts to correct disease-causing genetic mutations in humans, although generally successful, were tainted by several tragedies. In one instance, an eighteen-year-old male suffering from a partial deficiency of ornithine transcarboxylase (OTC) died after developing a massive inflammatory response to the genetic cargo delivery vehicle, an adenovirus vector, only four hours after receiving treatment.[153] However, the possibilities with CRISPR seem bright if we can improve our genomic understanding and the implications of this complex technology and how it may be harnessed as a tool to drive more precise, targeted treatments forward for better patient outcomes. But with CRISPR human trials no in effect, we're making progress and companies globally are investing.

150 GATLIN, ALLISON. 2018. "CRISPR Gene Editing And 3 Biotech Companies Blaze New Path To Cures | Stock News & Stock Market Analysis – IBD." Investor's Business Daily.

151 Lino, Christopher A., Jason C. Harper, James P. Carney, and Jerilyn A. Timlin. 2018. "Delivering CRISPR: A Review Of The Challenges And Approaches." Drug Delivery 25 (1): 1234-1257.

152 Ibid.

153 Ibid.

Of course, there isn't just one biotech company in the gene-editing race. In 2016—in addition to CRISPR Therapeutics—Intellia Therapeutics and Editas Medicine released their initial public offering to investors.[154] In 2018, two U.S. companies announced their partnership to launch a CRISPR gene-editing clinical trial in a German hospital.[155]

Two companies, Vertex Pharmaceuticals (based in Boston) and CRISPR Therapeutics (based in Switzerland), are hoping to study and treat the blood disease, β-thalassemia, which causes hemoglobin deficiencies.[156] The study will extract blood cells from patients, edit the gene *BCL11A*, and then inject or reintroduce them to the participants. This particular gene represses hemoglobin in infancy in a normal and healthy patient. So, by targeting the gene that represses hemoglobin production, the researchers hope they can help stimulate normal hemoglobin production in adults and offset the gene mutation behind the disease. In this approach, they are editing a healthy gene rather than editing the gene mutation causing the disease. This study demonstrates, in its approach, the complexity of the genome and how different genes work together. Through it we see how genes may suppress or express themselves to potentially offset the side effects or causes of a disease. The prediction with this study is that patients suffering from β-thalassemia and sickle cell

154 GATLIN, ALLISON. 2018. "CRISPR Gene Editing And 3 Biotech Companies Blaze New Path To Cures | Stock News & Stock Market Analysis – IBD." Investor's Business Daily.

155 "US Companies Launch CRISPR Clinical Trial." 2020. The Scientist Magazine®.

156 "A Safety And Efficacy Study Evaluating CTX001 In Subjects With Transfusion-Dependent B-Thalassemia – Full Text View – Clinicaltrials.gov." 2020. Clinicaltrials.gov.

disease will produce normal levels of hemoglobin after the repression of the *BCL11A* is lifted.[157]

According to Nessan Bermingham, former Chief Executive Officer at Intellia Therapeutics, as many as five thousand diseases could be cured with a single gene edit. The World Health Organization has released an even higher estimate, at ten thousand with a single gene edit.[158]

Intellia is partnering with Regeneron Pharmaceuticals to develop a therapy to treat transthyretin amyloidosis, which is characterized by the buildup of abnormal protein deposits throughout the body. [159] The treatment would use a CRISPR gene-editing approach: extract cells from the patient, make the gene edit, and then reinsert. Editas Medicine is working on a CRISPR gene-editing treatment for patients with Leber congenital amaurosis, a genetic disease resulting in vision loss at birth. Both Intellia and Editas aimed to begin human trials in 2018. [160] Genome engineered humans are not yet with us, but this idea is no longer distant future science fiction.

For example, a group of scientists in Philadelphia demonstrated they could use the CRISPR-Cas9 to remove HIV infection from human cells.[161] In 2016, Doudna predicted she would see clinical trials beginning, and even therapies. Then, in 2018, history was made when a physician in China claimed

---

157 Ibid.
158 "Genes And Human Diseases." 2020. World Health Organization.
159 "Pipeline – Intellia Therapeutics." 2020. Intellia Therapeutics.
160 "Editas Medicine." 2020. Editas Medicine. Dashi, Howard, 2017.
161 Sequential LASER ART and CRISPR Treatments Eliminate HIV-1 in a Subset of Infected Humanized Mic."

to have conducted a CRISPR-Cas9 gene edit on two human beings to make them resistant to contracting HIV.

He Jiankui, a Chinese physician, did clinical research conducting gene edits on fetuses. According to Jiankui, one couple in his clinical trial gave birth to a set of genetically engineered twins in whom the CCR5 gene had been eliminated, rendering them HIV resistant. Shortly after Jiankui's announcement, the world's second Human Genome Editing Summit was held in Hong Kong to discuss whether or not humans should begin genetically modifying themselves, and if so, how. After all, genetic edits in an embryo will be passed on to offspring and will eventually affect the entire gene pool.

In 2018, in Europe, patients with sickle cell anemia began enrolling in a CRISPR gene-editing study.[162] The FDA in the U.S. has approved the first CRISPR gene-editing study with the sponsorship of Vertex Pharmaceuticals and CRISPR Therapeutics.

According to geneticist Rodolphe Barrangou, early targets in humans for CRISPR application are liver and eye disease. These diseases are well understood, making them likely candidates for successful trials. Compared to solid tissues, using CRISPR gene-editing technologies in the blood or in eyes is relatively simple, making its application to eye diseases or disease of the blood a promising way to test effectiveness. Denser tissue studies, such as bone tissue, will come later.

---

162 Banks, Marcus, Greg Uyeno, Amy Nordrum, Jeanette Ferrara, Peter Hess, and Marcus Banks. 2018. "First CRISPR Clinical Trial Begins In Europe | Scienceline." Scienceline.

What this means for a patient like me, with a genetic eye disease, is that clinical studies using CRISPR may be at the forefront of this research.

Early success is needed in human trials to attract greater interest and investment in this expensive industry. Currently, gene-editing companies are seeking the shortest and most straight forward paths to clinical trial success.

The relative simplicity of CRISPR makes it appealing. We're still learning how to prevent, limit, and correct off-target edits of the technology. The explosion of CRISPR gene-editing technology is creating, new industries and jobs, like Bradley's.

A VISION FOR THE FUTURE OF CRISPR AND PRECISION MEDICINE

We're working on the delivery of CRISPR to cells and better understanding how DNA is repaired. This technology can be applied to adult and embryo cells alike, and the effects are only just beginning to be understood. Jennifer Doudna and Emmanuelle Charpentier have called together a global conversation to consider all the ethical and societal implications of this new technology.

In order for CRISPR to become a globally prescribed therapeutic approach, partnerships and combinations of industries and ideas—such as Bradley's intersection of computer science and biology—will need to be developed. Biotechnology and pharmaceutical companies with expertise in manufacturing with the ability to scale will be required for these therapies to have a broad impact and to develop treatments that can be distributed globally.

Many challenges remain in terms of understanding gene-editing implications. We have to be certain gene edits are done at the desired location to understand their implications and effects. We still have to develop methodologies for preventing immune responses that limit the in vivo administration of vectors or genome editing complexes. In short, the complexity is largely still in the actual delivery of the gene edit and ensuring it is precisely measured and accurate. We also still have to learn how making a gene edit will affect an individual's long-term health that of their potential offspring.

Insurers, gene therapy clinicians, and pharmaceutical and biotech companies will need to design and test new payment models for expensive but potentially curative therapies to patients in need. Gene therapies may well become part of our standard treatment for human disease. Though currently prohibitive in cost and regulation, these approaches should be accessible to more than the wealthiest. Once perfected, these treatments should be offered to multitudes of patients in need.

CHAPTER 9:

THE GOOGLE, MICROSOFT, AMAZON, AND APPLE ENTRANCE INTO GENOMICS AND PRECISION MEDICINE

─────

"Marked by the completion of the Human Genome project, life sciences entered the era of big data."

–CHINA NATIONAL GENEBANK[163]

BIOENGINEERING THE FUTURE

Modern technology has given us a new way to catalog and classify life, and to understand systematically how life organizes itself. Think of life's six kingdoms: animalia, plantae,

─────

163 GeneBank, China. 2020. "China National GeneBank." Cngb.org.

fungi, protista, archaebacteria, and eubacteria. First, these groups were organized by looking at physical characteristics. As science developed, we could understand and classify them by cell structure. Now with genomics, we can classify by genetic makeup. When inputting a genetic code into computers, we can predict with surprising accuracy what a person looks like, their age, their height, and their weight. We are only beginning to imagine what else our genetic codes may or may not reveal about us; we have to decide collectively as a society what it can mean for our future as a species.

THE SYSTEMS BIOLOGY MOVEMENT

George Church, Harvard professor and geneticist, helped launch the science of bioinformatics after working on the Human Genome Project. He is a believer in systematizing genomics to engineer our future. Currently, he is applying genomics to the development of a dating app called digiD8.[164] Church believes this could eliminate many diseases one day and could "biologically enhance" us. Voicing strong opposition to eugenics, Church insists he values genetic diversity. He believes that the app will address only a subset of the most severe genetic diseases, like Tay-Sachs or cystic fibrosis. Church's project, among many others combining big data and genetics, illustrates the various frontiers we are engineering.

Systems biology emerged as the result of the genetics catalog provided by the Human Genome Project, and a growing

---

164 Flynn, Megan. 2019. "A Harvard scientist is developing a DNA-based dating app." *The Washington Post.*

understanding of how genes and their resulting proteins give rise to biological form and function. Systems biology has influenced a new wave of scientists, like Church, aided by the internet and increased ability to store and distribute massive amounts of information. Couple this with advances in computing power, new research technologies like CRISPR, and the infusion of scientists from other disciplines such as computer scientists, mathematicians, physicists, and engineers. Systems biology, then, began with inventories and is developing as an interdisciplinary science. The era of big data is truly learning and living.

So, what is the difference between a computer code and a living code? How does the code work, and why does life replicate itself? These are the great questions of our era that the world's most powerful companies and governments are all trying to answer.

"The 'genetic program' unfolds through time in a consistent manner—it is not a program with an aim—it is merely there, and functions because it cannot do otherwise," wrote Antoine Danchin, a world-renowned geneticist and former director of Genomics and Genetics at Institut Cochin in Paris, France.[165]

---

165 Danchin, Antoine. 2009. "Bacteria as Computers Making Computers." FEMS Microbiology Reviews 33 (1): 3-26.

THE COMPLEXITY GROWS: LOOKING AT GENES COLLECTIVELY

The main goal of Antoine's research has been to understand how genes function collectively in the cell. Antoine argues that analyzing single genes limits our thinking and understanding of the magnificent portrait of the human body, and how all the pieces work together. Imagine Van Gogh's *Starry Night*. The individual, isolated brushstrokes cannot capture the paintings dynamic landscape. Similarly, examining a single gene does not illustrate its many relationships with the human body.

Antoine's vision recognizes the need for tremendous computing power to decipher the genome. In 1985, he started a collaboration with computer scientists to evaluate artificial intelligence techniques as applied to the study of integrated problems in molecular genetics.[166]

TURING MACHINES AND THE CONCEPT OF A GENETIC PROGRAM

Tech companies are approaching genetics in a way that Antoine has tried to make explicit—using the idea that cells behave as computers, or Turing Machines. A Turing Machine is a mathematical model of computation that defines an abstract machine.[167] The Turing Machine can read and write symbols on a strip of tape according to a table of rules.[168] Given any computer algorithm, or numeric instructions, a Turing Machine simulates the algorithm's

---

166 "Molecular Genetics." 2012.
167 Savage, John. "Models Of Computation: Exploring the Power of Computing." 1998.
168 Ibid.

logic. The Turing Machine operates on an infinite memory tape divided into discrete cells. The machine positions its "head" over a cell and "reads" or "scans" the symbol there.[169] Then, from the symbol and its finite list of instructions, the Turing Machine writes a corresponding symbol, like a digit or a letter, in the cell, and either moves the tape one cell left or right to proceed to a subsequent instruction.

So, can genetic instructions that express life be boiled down into a mathematical model like a Turing Machine? For "computers do not make computers. For cells to make cells requires a specific organization of the genetic program," wrote Antoine.[170]

Each human genome contains far more data than we can understand—approximately three billion genes. The difference between us and the rest of life is about five hundred genes. It has taken us over sixty years to understand about 1 percent of what the human genome means. Our biological code is thus too complex for us to ever understand without the help of artificial intelligence.

HOW TECH COMPANIES ARE APPROACHING GENOMICS

Imagine what other applications our genetic catalog could have in helping us make health decisions. Imagine you could swipe your genes at a drugstore while filling a prescription to match you with the most effective drug. As you walk down the grocery aisle, a rolling inventory of

---

169 Ibid.
170 Danchin, Antoine. 2009. "Bacteria as Computers Making Computers." FEMS Microbiology Reviews 33 (1): 3-26.

genetic data could help you select or avoid certain food choices. Now that we can generate genomes quickly and cheaply, who is better positioned to apply machine learning to genetics? Can we trust AI and algorithms to try to decipher the code of life?

Some of the world's most powerful companies are investing in the idea of likening the genetic code to computer codes, or "the living software revolution." Microsoft, Google, IBM, and Amazon now have genomics, health, and life sciences programs and are investing billions in the living data era to biologically engineer our future.

They are talking about rates of technology, the explosion of data, and the rise in artificial intelligence capabilities—all of which we can broadly term Moore's Law. Moore's perception was that the number of transistors on a microchip doubles every two years, though the cost of computers is halved. Thus, technological growth is and continues to be exponential.

In the genetics explosion of the last two decades, our ability to quickly and cost effectively sequence the human genome has outpaced even Moore's Law and surpassed our own expectations about our abilities to gather this data.

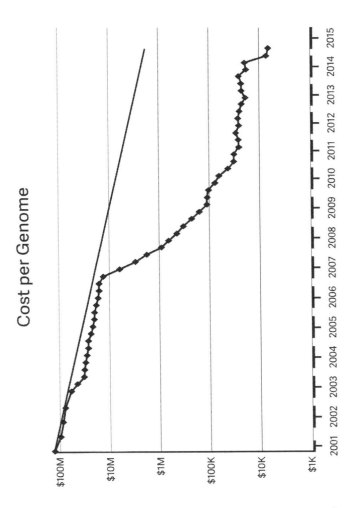

The cost of sequencing a genome over time—image courtesy of Genome.gov[171]

Despite this challenge to understandmost genes individually—mostly not considering the dimension of understanding

---

171 "Human Genome Project FAQ." 2020. Genome.gov.

genes collectively—the demand for genomics programs and sequencing for individuals, companies, and governments is growing. Some estimate genomics sequencing market size to reach $87 billion by 2023 as part of the Precision Medicine trend. [172]

The common goal among many of these initiatives is to understand to what extent genetics, behaviors, and environment influence human health, with broader goals of implementing a patient or population-specific treatment intervention. This is a problem we can't solve without the help of lots of smart computing power and connecting our ideas and discoveries together.

We were working in information silos in the pre-internet era, before our ability to exchange ideas and information and connect thinking around the world exploded. Like only looking at a single gene, we too were once the single stars in Van Gogh's *Starry Night.* Now, our collective web of ideas is connecting and working together, painting an ever more magnificent canvas. Think of what our knowledge and discovery web will look like for plugging in our genomics data into a shared gene bank to include health information, with the help of machine learning and heavy computing power constantly updating and constantly learning from new information in real time.

---

172 Inc., Global. 2020. "Precision Medicine Market Size To Exceed $87 Billion By 2023: Global Market Insights Inc." Prnewswire.com.

GENOMICS IS IN THE CLOUD: AI AND ANALYTICS TOOLS

By having your genome sequenced with a high degree of accuracy and plugging it into the cloud in a globally connected inventory, you can contribute to this global genomics conversation. When working with data at this scale, it is very difficult to collaborate on projects that have to navigate and work across multiple global institutions. Scientists working on and studying diseases aren't generally located in the same places geographically. Without cloud capabilities, disk drives have to be shipped around the world to share this information. Another challenge in analyzing the data sets is the time it takes to perform the computing analysis on them; using local resources can take days to weeks. However, through the use of cloud computing, we may derive meaningful answers and exchanges of ideas more quickly.

Antoine's vision is being realized, and AI and machine learning are helping researchers make sense of all of this genetics data as we become more open to sharing and compiling it. One estimate argues that having everyone's genome sequenced could extend lifespans on average five to ten years.[173] We could know which drugs will and won't work, our susceptibility to disease, and habits to note in our daily living and health.

Seeing the competitive advantage of machine learning and sheer computing power, tech companies have raced into the genetics sequencing market, all with different applications of the genetics data. They're combining genetic data with information about health and lifestyle, smoking, nutritional intake,

---

173   Resnick, Richard. 2020. "Transcript Of "Welcome To The Genomic Revolution"." Ted.com.

fitness, and other habits. This is something we've never been able to do before. Here's an overview of the work and investments they're making to push precision medicine forward:

WHAT TECH (AND PHARMA) COMPANIES ARE DOING ABOUT IT, AND WHY WE NEED THEM

IBM'S FAMOUS WATSON

IBM's Watson Health Platform, an AI tool, is being used to extract unstructured data from peer-reviewed medical literature to "learn" and continually grow its knowledge base. It provides information on the latest approved clinical options, including targeted and immunotherapy options, genomic databases, and relevant publications.

So, after a patient's DNA is sequenced, IBM Watson for Genomics processes and analyzes the information. For a cancer patient, a sample of the tumor from the patient can be added to this genetic profile. Watson will then provide a summary of the tumor's profile, highlighting the mutations in the tumor cells differing from healthy cells, and provide therapeutic options that might be most effective against these cancerous cells. This helps the physician identify the tumor's "driver mutation." By pulling information from available literature added to its database, the molecular profile analysis can show mutations that are relevant to the patient's cancer case. Evidence levels of each therapeutic option can be displayed to the physician, and clinical trial data can be reviewed and accessed. Learn more by checking out the Watson for Genomics Website.[174]

---

174 "IBM Watson For Genomics – Overview – United States." 2020. Ibm.com.

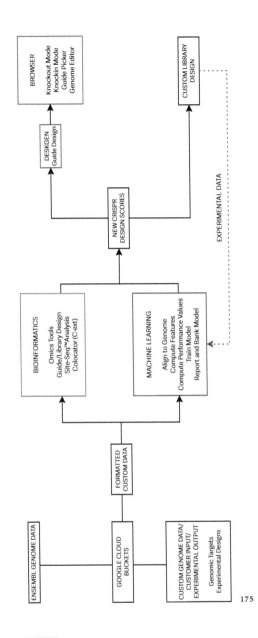

175 Inc., Global. 2020. "Precision Medicine Market Size To Exceed $87 Billion By 2023: Global Market Insights Inc." Prnewswire.com.

First, experimental or reference data is uploaded to Google Cloud. It is then formatted and processed before moving to bioinformatics and machine learning teams. Using this data, they can analyze and design CRISPR experiments or develop new models. This leads new CRISPR designs which can then be tested in the lab, tested, and provide feedback to implement into future models.

GOOGLE'S VERILY, ALL OF US, AND PROJECT BASELINE

Google has been foraying into life sciences for a decade. First launched as X Development LLC, then called Google X, their initial venture was a somewhat secretive attempt to apply Google's technologies to life sciences. Google X defines itself as an organization to invest in and launch "moonshot" projects that aim to make the world a radically better place.

In 2015, Google renamed its life science division "Verily." In January 2019, Verily raised over two billion dollars in capital, leading the biotech industry in raised funds. Verily's CEO talks about the company's future as one that is increasingly flexible and expansive in its focus areas with multiple divisions.[176]

Verily has initiated a number of projects combining artificial intelligence with big data to monitor, improve, predict, and better understand health. One example is their Study Watch program. Study Watch is an effort to create an investigation

---

176 "Xconomy: Alphabet's Biotech R&D Arm Verily Raises $1B To Fuel Growth." 2019. Xconomy.

medical device to seamlessly gather data for clinical studies conducted by Verily. The watch gathers physiological and environmental data with always-on specialized sensors to wear continuously for long-term data collection. This could significantly impact clinical trials for new drugs and devices.

Rather than scheduling days for patients to commute for routine testing (like I did when trying to enroll in clinical trials), data could be more objectively gathered in greater quantities in real time. This could potentially expedite clinical trial processes and reduce much of the capital and time invested in data collection.

Smart Watch is the tool being used to gather and collect data from participants in their Project Baseline study. "We are taking a long-range view in life sciences and healthcare, and Baseline is a way to start to look for observations that could provide a reference set for a new set of tools and technologies," said Jessica Mega, Verily's Chief Medical Officer.[177]

Project Baseline focuses on understanding and studying "what a healthy human should be" by attempting to establish a baseline for good health. The study combines patients' genomes with information from wearables like Smart Watch to create a picture of the healthy human. The Baseline project debut has over ten thousand study participants and is tracking their health over four years.[178] By tracking participants' lifestyle activities over a period of

177 "Xconomy: Alphabet's Biotech R&D Arm Verily Raises $1B To Fuel Growth." 2019. Xconomy.

178 Wiggers, Kyle. 2019. "Alphabet's Verily Raises $1 Billion To Make Health Care Smarter." Venturebeat.

years, we may become much closer to understanding and answering these questions than where we are today. We could also understand how a person transitions from a healthy state to illness.

MICROSOFT GENOMICS

Microsoft, too, has entered the genetics foray, with its program Microsoft Genomics.[179] Microsoft Genomics is bringing Microsoft's Azure Cloud to genomics computation. They've developed a Genome Analysis Toolkit to help researchers analyze genomic data sets. In partnership with Stanford University, Microsoft has also developed a new genomics algorithm on an Intel Altera field programmable gene array infrastructure with cloud computing, applying machine learning capabilities to deciphering, analyzing, and understanding genomics data. They've termed some of their investment "the living software revolution."[180]

Microsoft is attempting to learn how to program cells, rather than computers alone. Like inputting 1s and 0s to run a computer program, altering the genetic code will change how the program runs. By developing a living software compiler and translating high-level biological processes into their inputs of the A(adenine), T(thymine), G(guanine), and C(cytosine), in theory, we can program cells to perform certain actions. Rather than guessing how a patient may respond to treatment through trial and error,

---

179 "Microsoft Genomics." 2020. Microsoft Genomics.
180 "YouTube." 2020. YouTube.com.

the theory is that one day we will be able to know or program a patient's cells to respond a certain way to diseases and medicines. Microsoft poses these new possibilities and questions: "What if we could program our cells to detect or eradicate disease, or replace damaged tissue? That would mean longer, healthier lives. Programming biology allows us to revolutionize medicine on a global scale."[181]

This thinking at Microsoft builds on the 2012 Nobel Prize of Medicine winners John B. Gurdon and Shinya Yamanaka for their discovery that mature cells can be reprogrammed to become immature cells capable of developing into all tissues of the body.[182] A similar discovery was also made, reprogramming stem cells back to their embryonic state.

Station B at Microsoft is working to answer these very questions to learn how to program biology more effectively with an integrated system. Microsoft used their Design Solver program, used for conventional software verification, to uncover cells' internal genetic program, and use the program to accelerate progress back to cells' stem-like state and determine which genes were critical to do this and which genes turned on and off over time. This computer model could tell scientists in advance what would otherwise take decades to uncover. [183]

181 Techmash! View. 2019. "Microsoft Innovation Stories! The Living Software Revolution!" Techmash.
182 "The Nobel Prize In Physiology Or Medicine 2012." 2020. Nobelprize.org.
183 Techmash! View. 2019. "Microsoft Innovation Stories! The Living Software Revolution!" Techmash.

AMAZON HEALTH AND LIFE SCIENCES

Initially driven by identifying new ways to keep their employees healthy and lower spending on insurance, Amazon developed a three-segment health and life sciences division:

- Healthcare providers and payers
- Pharma and biotech
- Genomics

The division is building partnerships with healthcare institutions using cloud technology and machine learning. Ensuring that the three sectors can share data and collaborate, I think, is where we as patients, consumers, drug developers, and providers can all benefit. Amazon's health and life sciences customers include Illumina, the Centers for Disease Control, healthcare.gov, DNAnexus, Celgene, the Cleveland Clinic, Bristol Myers Squibb, and Allergan.[184]

As the world's largest cloud provider, Amazon Web Services (AWS) develops cloud solutions for companies and organizations in the business of sequencing and storing genomics data. AWS is also working on the 1000 Genomes Project, an international collaboration that has established the most detailed cataloger of human genetic variation.[185] They are making the data publicly available to the community, free of charge, which is where learning and discovery can happen for researchers.[186]

---

184 "Healthcare And Life Sciences On AWS." 2020. Amazon Web Services, Inc.

185 "1000 Genomes Project And AWS." 2020. Amazon Web Services, Inc.

186 "Healthcare And Life Sciences On AWS." 2020. Amazon Web Services, Inc

APPLE HEALTH APPS

Apple is trying to make the iPhone[187] and its other devices integral to digital health. Their Health app has more than seventy different types of health data, and they've begun trying to build apps to assist healthcare professionals as well. Apple is also getting involved with studies collecting DNA, in particular one planned by UC San Francisco to study causes of premature birth.[188]

ASIMOV

Asimov, a synthetic biology company, has a mission is to "build a genetic design platform to establish the next generation of therapeutics and molecular manufacturing."[189] Founded by a team of MIT biological engineers, they have created a programming language that allows them to rapidly design complex DNA-encoded circuits to give new functions to living cells. They are also building an industry-grade computer-aided design and genetic engineering platform to engineer living cells.[190]

PALANTIR

Palantir is a data science and analytics company that has partnered on significant U.S. government projects, such as tracking Osama bin Laden. Palantir has a contract with the NIH in the National Center for Advanced Translational

---

187 Regalado, Antonio. 2020. "Exclusive: Apple Pursues DNA Data." MIT Technology Review.

188 Ibid.

189 "Asimov — Intelligent Design." 2020. Asimov.Io.

190 "Asimov — Intelligent Design." 2020. Asimov.Io.

Sciences (NCATS). Palantir's software will be used to combine proprietary and public data into one interface—combining screening, genomics, and other high throughput biological data integrated onto one platform to "get more treatments to patients more quickly."[191]

GENETICS POWER IS IN THE CLOUD

Competing companies and governments are building their own health and genomics databases. However, these entities are increasingly migrating data into digital clouds. Ultimately, there are only four major cloud providers—IBM, Amazon AWS (the largest), Microsoft Azure (second in size, but half the size of AWS), and Google Drive.[192] So despite different companies, governments, and cloud providers resisting data sharing between one another, it will all eventually be migrated, most likely and hopefully, into *one cloud*.

Tech companies have superior abilities and resources to ensure data privacy and protection. All four of these companies are investing heavily in machine learning, genomics programs, and creating synergies with related health and life sciences divisions. They will only increase in significance to developing new drugs, assisting physicians in diagnosis, evaluation, and treatment decisions, and generating imagined and unimagined insights into genomics and what it means for our health, the present, and our future as a species. They will launch the "living software revolution."

---

191 WIRE, BUSINESS. 2018. "National Institutes Of Health Awards Palantir With Contract To Advance Critical Health Research." Businesswire.com.

192 Olanubi, Sijuola. 2016. "Top Five Largest Cloud Companies In The World – Tharawat Magazine." Tharawat Magazine.

CONCLUSION

Combining and sharing this data ethically and responsibly could have miraculous implications for the future of human health and value-based care, personalized for each patient. What we can see is the emergence of partnerships between pharmaceutical and tech companies, governments, universities, and non-profits—all creating new synergies needed to bioengineer the future.

Many of us are skeptical about the ethical use of our health and genomics data, but this data is necessary as fuel for the precision medicine future. One business model to navigate data privacy boundaries and laws could be for patients to own, view, and, if they choose, sell their genomics and health data. In many cases, hospitals and research groups are legally bound to hold their medical data. But, technically, no law yet stops individuals from sharing and selling their data by choice. This may be the rationale behind the "empowering patients" rhetoric. Putting consumers in control by giving them ownership of their data may be the fastest vehicle forward.

PART 3:

WHY INVEST IN PRECISION MEDICINE?

CHAPTER 10:

A MORE PRECISE APPROACH TO CANCER: FRANCOIS'S STORY

"I was treated at one of the U.S.'s best hospitals, and I was astonished. In many ways the U.S. is far ahead of the rest of the world, and in many ways behind. Your healthcare system, compared to France, is far behind."

−FRANCOIS GENDRE, PHD, MOLECULAR

BIOLOGIST AND DIPLOMAT

Francois Gendre, a friend of mine, was born in Lyon, France. In 2016, Francois was diagnosed with a squamous cell carcinoma cancer in the U.S. He was working as a diplomat at the French Embassy in Washington, D.C. Prior to knowing Francois, I'd had little experience with cancer. Seeing his diagnosis, treatment, and outcome both in France and in the U.S., however, profoundly influenced me and my perspectives on the French and U.S. healthcare systems.

Francois believed in scientific frontiers and in driving new immunotherapies and targeted gene therapies forward. He knew while receiving traditional treatments—chemotherapy, surgery, and radiation—that new and better treatments were being theorized and developed. He didn't give up that hope while being blasted with a variety of toxic and painful cancer treatments, and he passed this hope on to me. This is why I share Francois's story with you and why I believe in and see the biopharma future. Through witnessing Francois's struggle, I realized much of the research being done in genetics and precision medicine has made a significant impact in developing innovative cancer therapies.

At age eighteen, Francois began pursuing his studies in molecular biology, going on to earn two master's degrees and a PhD. His research began in the late 1970s and early 1980s, when gene editing was becoming more widely used in research and laboratory testing. Francois realized there was a significant opportunity in the commercial application of laboratory gene-editing research. He thus began working as a molecular biologist in the food industry.

He began his career with Carlsberg, a brewing company. There, he developed new strains of yeast to increase efficiencies in the fermentation process for the beer industry. Quickly realizing his own talent, he continued applying his interests in genetics and molecular biology in the food industry at Danone, eventually climbing to Head of Global Scientific Research. He developed a new strain of bacteria to further increase the rate at which fermentation in yogurt products could occur, thereby increasing the efficiency of the yogurt-making process. He began traveling around the world for his work.

In his forties, Francois was diagnosed with leukemia. He overcame the diagnosis but continued to be diagnosed with cancer over six times in his life. Continuing to defeat the cancer, Francois leveraged his scientific brilliance, business charisma, and global outlook to become a scientific attaché at the French Embassy in Washington, D.C. His mission was to build partnerships and collaborations between the U.S. and French scientific communities. His English was perfect, but difficult for the average Washingtonian to understand.

Just after my Peace Corps service in Azerbaijan and Georgia, I moved to Washington, D.C. and began teaching English on the side. Francois was my first client. Francois opened up my mind to the world of global business and to thinking about the strong potential and future of gene therapy and CRISPR applications to human health with precision medicine.

"Doctors will have a cure for your eyes in your lifetime," he used to say. "I'm sure of it. Give it ten years." After being told for most of my life there was nothing that could be done, I had mostly given up on a cure.

Francois told me he dreamed his whole life of coming to the U.S. "To be free to do what I want, despite Americans having many problems," he said. "It's strange—in some ways you Americans are so ahead, and in others so far behind, like your healthcare system."

Traveling to conferences in San Francisco and visiting the Google facility in Silicon Valley, Francois speculated about the future of technology around the world, and the United States' role in driving it forward. He wrote papers about this speculative future and the increasing role of artificial intelligence in an interconnected global and digital world. He helped me imagine what this future might look like.

Six months into knowing Francois, he told me that he had been to the dentist for surgery. "I went back several times—it doesn't seem to be healing," he said. "The dentist said it's nothing, to just use mouthwash." Visiting Spain, Francois went to a second dentist to get another opinion. The dentists discovered the cause of the wound that wasn't healing. The source was a cancerous tumor, growing beneath his tooth.

Francois called me that afternoon in shock. "The dentist here said it is cancer, and I must have it removed immediately," he said. "Perhaps I can have the procedure done at Georgetown—I hear it has a very good reputation."

A week later, Francois had his first surgery in an attempt to remove the tumor. His physician in D.C. had diagnosed the cancer as stage one to two and told Francois it wasn't a serious procedure and should take no more than two hours. "I'm not concerned," said the surgeon. "I'm very confident we can lead you to a good outcome."

I stopped by the hospital the evening of his surgery, three hours after it had begun. The nurse told me Francois was still in surgery, assuring me everything would be fine. After six hours of anesthesia and surgery, the doctor said the surgery was finished. Francois was in a great deal of pain, despite being under many anesthetics, and was hooked up to a feeding tube. He wasn't sure what time it was. "How long was I in surgery?" he asked. I looked out the window, realizing how late at night it was under a full, pale moon. "Six hours," I said. Francois straightened in his hospital gown, eyebrows raised.

"Why did it take so long?" he asked. "The doctor assured me it was two hours, that it was nothing." I heard the worry in his voice. I, too, had my own questions.
"I'm not sure," I said. "I'll come by in the morning and we can speak with the doctor then."
Francois squeezed my hand.
"Thank you," he said.

I returned early the next morning. Francois was more distressed than the evening before, less groggy, and more alert. He was still waiting for answers from the doctor. "I don't understand—why isn't he here?" he asked. The nurse assured us the doctor was coming soon, that we shouldn't worry. We waited another hour, worrying as we watched seconds pass before us.

Later that day, Francois called with bad news. "The doctor says I must have another surgery tomorrow morning to be sure the cancer is removed. I am concerned it is serious, or the doctor has done something wrong." I returned to the hospital. Francois pulled the thin white hospital sheet over his lap and held my hand. The doctor stepped into the room to give an update on his decision.

"This is a tricky cancer," said the doctor. "I went home last night thinking about the surgery. I wanted to put you back into surgery this morning to be sure I removed all the cancer." "I don't understand," said Francois. "You already cut more than you said, taking four of my teeth—the surgery lasted for six hours instead of two." The doctor frowned.

"I want to be sure we remove all the cancerous tissue," he added carefully. "I don't want it to relapse." Francois crossed his arms.

"I trust you. You're the expert." The doctor looked back at his chart, brow furrowed.

An hour later, Francois underwent a second surgery, this time several more teeth removed as well as part of his jawbone. Francois was discharged from the hospital several days later. He was prescribed a strictly liquid diet for two weeks and radiation therapy for six weeks. He had lost much of the sensation in the left side of his mouth.

The following week, Francois showed me his medical bills from the surgery, having spent three days in the hospital, and with good insurance from the embassy. "$125,000 is the bill—I'm supposed to pay $20,000," exclaimed Francois. "How does your medical system work, and where are the numbers coming from?" I knew hospital visits were always expensive but had no price tag reference for surgery in the U.S. or Europe.

After Francois's surgery and six weeks of radiation therapy, eight months passed and his physician didn't call. He hadn't scheduled a check-up appointment to see if the surgery was healing. Scarred and in considerable pain, Francois was still struggling to eat solid food. The left side of his face was swollen and red, the tissue struggling to heal from surgery followed by radiation therapy.

"In France, it is mandatory for the physician to do imaging every two months following cancer treatment to catch a potential relapse early in the process," said Francois. "I don't understand how your system works." I didn't understand either.

Eight months after the radiation therapy had ended, Francois went back to Georgetown to have a second round of imaging. The cancer had returned. Despite the devastating news, Francois remained confident he could overcome it.

Despite his confidence, Francois was nevertheless upset with his treatment at a renowned U.S. hospital and by the confusing, costly medical bills (which he refused to pay out of principle). He decided to have a second surgery performed in his native hometown in France, in a system he understood.

Following Francois's next round of surgery, I visited him in Lyon, France. He was pleased with the results and thought the surgeon had done a superior job. He remained confident and strong that this time, the cancerous tissue had been fully removed.

Francois hadn't received this kind of follow-up care in the U.S., and if he had, it would have been extraordinarily expensive. They had just given him a packet of paper with instructions and told him to stay on a liquid diet for two weeks. In

France, the nurse gave him recipes and ideas for how and what to cook to return to health. Each day, a nurse visited his home to clean and dress his wounds—all free of charge under the French system.

Francois seemed to be healing well, and on his way to recovery. Though in pain and with difficulty in eating, Francois was optimistic in spirit that he would recover. He returned weeks after his surgery to the U.S. to resume his work at the embassy and resumed his English lessons. He had new difficulty in speaking and being understood, especially by strangers.

"Do you know how much my surgery cost in France?" he asked.
"How much?" I asked.
"Twenty Euros—can you believe it?"

After his surgery in Washington, D.C., Francois had been prescribed an array of expensive painkillers and medication to increase saliva production and help him manage food, all of which Francois found ineffective and costly. The price of one box of SalivaMAX, a relatively simple compound to stimulate saliva production, was $1,000.

Once more, however, Francois's cancer relapsed. He had another surgery performed in France. Again, only weeks later, he returned to D.C. to work, this time in more pain and with less optimism. He started speaking to me about alternative cancer therapies that were still in clinical trials in France. "We are working to develop immunotherapies," he said. "They would inject the tumor with cells to work as a therapy. It's more targeted, and precise. But we will have to wait to see."

After his third surgery, the damaged tissue from radiation and the previous two surgeries wasn't healing. I accompanied Francois to the ER to inquire about the open wound. We waited for over an hour, went back to the patient rooms, and waited to see a physician. Francois was seen by three physicians. Each time, they asked the same questions. Who was his overseeing physician in Washington, D.C.? (Francois's overseeing physician had left). How many surgeries had he had performed, and what was the outcome of each? Who had prescribed radiation therapy? It was clear they were uncomfortable recommending treatment with his mixed records in their own hospital, and lack of records on hand from the follow-up treatment he had received in France. Francois became frustrated.

"All I want to know is if you can redo my stitches," he said. The physician couldn't agree, but it took them several hours to reach this decision.

"We cannot redo the stitches because the chance of infection may be quite high," they said. "We don't have your complete medical history, so we are concerned about treating you." The ER sent Francois home with instructions for packing his wound. "You can also come to the hospital to have assistance with packing it," they said. Francois asked about the price.

"Oh, we don't deal with that here. We work with another company to provide that service. I can't give you any information on that," they said. "You'll have to go to the other part of the building to find out." Francois and I left the hospital after hours of waiting and no clear course ahead for treatment or for his stitches. Francois decided he would no longer receive care in the U.S. and returned to France.

"I'm not sure I'll come back," he said.

I visited Francois three more times in France. Each time he was weaker, had lost weight, and was in more pain. Eventually, the doctors decided they couldn't perform more surgery. After two rounds of unsuccessful chemotherapy, Francois still hung on to the hope that he could participate in an immunotherapy experimental trial. He never gave up, even in the days before his death.

On April 17, 2018, Francois passed away. His total treatment counts were two rounds of chemotherapy, four surgeries, and continual radiation therapy. All were unable to cure the cancer, which eventually began overtaking part of his face and neck. The rest of his body, however, was healthy.

"It's puzzling," said his final doctor in France. "He has only one part of his body with the cancer, and the rest of his body is quite fine and healthy. And yet, we cannot win."

Francois's battle with cancer in France and in the U.S. opened my mind to many issues in healthcare. It led to a better understanding of what cancer is, how it can quickly spread, and how lethal it may be. It also opened my mind to where we are in our scientific understanding, treatment, and diagnosis of cancer.

Here are some of my final observations from this experience:

- The French medical system's care, on average, is superior to the U.S. The difference in care I observed was particularly noticeable in follow-up processes and consistent evaluation of and attention to patients.
- All of Francois's treatments for three surgeries, two rounds of chemotherapy, months in and out of the hospital, and home visits from the nurse cost less than 1,000 Euros with the European Union's public option. The cost of a single surgery in the U.S. for Francois, and three days in the hospital (with the best insurance) was still $25,000 out of pocket.
- The French healthcare system, according to the World Health Organization, is ranked first globally, combining a variety of metrics. The U.S. system, under the same criteria, is ranked thirty-seventh globally.
- Our scientific understanding of cancer is still quite limited. Our approach to cancer, until very recently, has been the Vietnam approach. In this approach, with surgery, you remove what looks like a cancerous area, perform imaging, taking additional tissue samples throughout the surgery. The doctor checks the margins, or areas around the tumor, to see if the tissue appears to be cancerous and continues surgery if it doesn't appear healthy. Much of this is guesswork and practice—not hard science. With chemotherapy, a patient's body is flooded with chemicals that are toxic not only to cancerous cells but also to healthy cells. Hopefully in the process, the cancerous cells will be eliminated.
- Witnessing someone experience chemotherapy was one of the most emotionally taxing experiences of my life.

Francois lost over forty pounds and most of his hair, was sick to his stomach, and was emotionally demoralized each time he went into the hospital. It would take him several days to begin to recover and step out of bed after one round. Gradually, he became weaker and weaker.

- In radiation therapy, a patient's general tumor area is blasted with radiation waves. The radiation again destroys many healthy cells in the process of attempting to eradicate cancerous cells. You are blasting an area with a "bomb" of radiation.
- Francois again experienced a great deal of pain from the radiation therapy, which permanently damaged much of his tissue. In combination with surgery, his tissue lost the ability to heal and repair itself.
- Cancer cells can divide an unlimited number of times, while healthy cells are programmed to destroy themselves after a certain number of replications. In the process of these cancerous cells replicating, the gene sequence may again be altered, causing multiple genetic sequences of cancerous cells. This makes treating cancer especially difficult. On average for a patient to be diagnosed with cancer, there is a threshold of a minimum of six mutations different from the penitents' original genomic sequence. The result? Some cancerous cells may respond to a treatment while others don't. Those that don't continue replicating and growing. Treating cancer effectively is thus especially challenging.
- Our ability to tailor cancer treatments for patients and combine a variety of treatment options and approaches is improving, as are cancer recovery rates. Francois's fixation on an immunotherapy treatment option is one area

where we have seen the most success and potential in the precision medicine movement, which could've changed his outcomes.

WHY INVEST IN IMPROVING CANCER CARE

Francois's story, I think, gives a personal account for why we should invest in innovative cancer therapies. It's likely that many of us will either experience it ourselves or experience someone close to us being diagnosed with cancer. The NIH estimates that as many as one in three people will develop some form of cancer in their lifetime. Existing commonly prescribed treatments have low success rates for many patients and are—like the Vietnam approach—often imprecise.

There is hope on the horizon, however, with a precision medicine approach. By having the patient's genome sequenced or sequencing the cancerous cells, we can better identify mutations. Through sequencing thousands of patient genomes, we can also begin to recognize and even predict which genes may be more likely or more prone to mutation leading to cancer.

So, too, does examining how we've improved over time. A snapshot of the past and present of cancer tells us why we should continue researching and investing in new cancer therapies and believe in the potential to develop better medicines for cancer.

In 1976, the U.S. incidence rate for cancer was 400 cases for every 100,000 people, or less than half of 1 percent. The cancer mortality rate was 199 for every 100,000 people, or nearly 50 percent.[193] In the mid-1960s, clinical investigations of combination chemotherapy—using multiple drugs and different methods for treating cancer—were just beginning. Clinical studies of anticancer vaccines hadn't yet begun.[194]

What we've seen in near present terms is an improvement in care and patient outcomes, but an increase in the number of patients diagnosed with cancer annually. In 2007, the U.S. incidence for cancer was 461 patients per 100,000 people.[195] Some of this increase, however, can be attributed to an aging population in the U.S., and earlier diagnosis. Cancer death rates for patients have been declining since 1991. Among adults, the five-year relative rate for all cancers combined is now 68 percent.[196] The survival rate for children diagnosed with cancer since 2007, with all cancers combined, is about 81 percent.[197] Much of this progress in survival rates can be attributed to a better and more accurate diagnosis of cancer in patients.

In terms of considering treatment options for cancer, we've seen significant shifts in thinking. Combination chemotherapy has become a standard for treating many types of cancer and has shown higher success rates than one singular form of chemotherapy. Again, think back to the fact that different cancer cells may have different genetic sequences from one another, so some cancer cells may be destroyed from one

---

193 "Cancer Statistics." 2018. National Cancer Institute.
194 Ibid.
195 Ibid.
196 Ibid.
197 Ibid.

type of chemotherapy, while the others are not destroyed and continue to multiply and spread.

The National Human Genome Institute and the National Cancer Institute have combined forces to develop the Cancer Genome Atlas Program. The idea is that this combined research and repository of information on twenty cancers and the genes they are associated with will greatly enhance our understanding. We will hopefully be able to identify molecular changes to target in treatment, or even detect the cancer occurrence earlier and begin preemptive treatments. Many scientists, researchers, and physicians think this is key to better cancer treatments and outcomes.

CHAPTER 11:

APPLYING GENOMICS TO CANCER AND CAR T-CELL THERAPY

———

"Cancer patients successfully treated with immune checkpoint blockades are living proof of the power of basic science, of following our urge to learn and to understand how things work."
—*JIM ALLISON, NOBEL PRIZE WINNER*[198]

Cancer is one of the most widely diagnosed diseases in the world. Most of us have a family member or friend affected by some form of cancer. The World Health Organization estimates that as much as 30 percent of the world's population will contract some form of cancer during their lifetime.[199] It can also be one of the most difficult to treat. The causes of cancer are multiplicative—ranging from genetic factors to

---

198 "MD Anderson Immunologist Jim Allison Awarded Nobel Prize." 2020. MD Anderson Cancer Center.

199 "Cancer Statistics." 2018. National Cancer Institute.

the environment in which we live, to lifestyle, to chemical exposure. The greatest challenges in fighting cancer are that the disease comes from our own cells and that no two cancers in patients are the same, even when affecting the same organ.

All of the cells in a body, while being differentiated in function and type, have the same genetic sequence. What's different, then, about cancerous cells is that they contain a genetic mutation from a cell's original DNA sequence. This mutation causes the cancerous cells to grow differently, have different metabolic levels, and act in a way that is independent from the rest of the body's cells. They multiply faster, can divide indefinitely, and grow more quickly.

PRECISION MEDICINE AND CANCER TREATMENTS

Dr. Victor Li, a PhD researcher who worked on the Human Genome Project, spoke with me about historical and contemporary approaches to treating cancer. He said, "Treating cancer was like bombing Vietnam—throwing firepower and chemicals at an enemy that is difficult to see. Until now, we had this approach to cancer."

According to the NIH, surgery, chemotherapy, and radiation therapy are the most common types of cancer treatments available in most hospitals today.[200] Radiation therapy directs harmful radiation waves to a cancerous area in hopes of destroying the cancerous cells. Chemotherapy floods

---

200 Arruebo, Manuel, Nuria Vilaboa, Berta Sáez-Gutierrez, Julio Lambea, Alejandro Tres, Mónica Valladares, and África González-Fernández. 2011. "Assessment Of The Evolution Of Cancer Treatment Therapies." Cancers 3 (3): 3279-3330.

the body with toxic chemicals. Surgery attempts to physically remove a tumor and all surrounding cancerous cells. While in some cases effective, cancer treatments haven't been precise, sometimes leaving cancerous cells behind and resulting in relapse after treatment and destroying many healthy cells in the process.

Some of the most significant advances in the biotech and genomics industry are being applied to cancer therapy treatments. A new wave of cancer treatments has emerged that apply principles from genomics: immunotherapy, Car T-cell therapy, and cellular-based therapies. We've become better and more precise in treating and diagnosing patients with this difficult-to-treat disease. But we're just at the beginning.

IMMUNOTHERAPY IS MAKING PROGRESS IN CANCER TREATMENT

Car T-cell and immunotherapies use the body's own natural immunity to detect mutated cells. Immunotherapy uses the patient's own immune system to destroy tumors, and gene therapies are also showing progress in a precision approach to cancer treatment.[201]

In 2017, the FDA approved Kymriah (tisagenlecleucel) for certain pediatric and young adult patients with a form of acute lymphoblastic leukemia (ALL). "We're entering a new frontier in medical innovation with the ability to reprogram

---

201 Arruebo, Manuel, Nuria Vilaboa, Berta Sáez-Gutierrez, Julio Lambea, Alejandro Tres, Mónica Valladares, and África González-Fernández. 2011. "Assessment Of The Evolution Of Cancer Treatment Therapies." Cancers 3 (3): 3279-3330.

a patient's own cells to attack a deadly cancer," said FDA Commissioner Scott Gottlieb.[202]

With precision medicine and an enhanced understanding of the human genome, we are developing therapies such as Car T-cell therapies and can directly target cancerous cells.

Antibodies may be lower in toxicity and can provide specificity when targeting a cancerous tumor. Dr. Ronald Pepin is one researcher that began working on a more precise approach to cancer treatment.

CANCER TREATMENT SUMMARY TABLE

Cancer Therapy Overview			
Therapy	How It Works	Side Effects	Limitations
Surgery	Surgically remove the tumor	Removal of healthy tissue surrounding the tumor, complications from surgery	Cannot target metastasized cells
Radiation	Damages the DNA of cancerous cells	Damage to healthy cells resulting in more cancerous cells	Expensive in the long term
Chemotherapy	Targets rapidly dividing cells (mostly cancer cells)	Hair loss, intestinal damage, nausea	Cancer cells develop resistance to chemotherapy, not specific

---

202 "FDA Approval Brings First Gene Therapy To The United States." 2018. U.S. Food And Drug Administration.

Targeted therapy	Targets proteins required for cancer growth	Liver problems, diarrhea, skin rash	Cancer cells develop resistance
Immunotherapy	Use patient's immune system against cancer	Autoimmune effects	Tailored and expensive

RONALD PEPIN'S VIEWS ON IMMUNOTHERAPY AND ITS BEGINNINGS: BRISTOL MYERS SQUIBB, MEDAREX, AND PD1 ANTIBODIES

Ronald grew up in Bedford, Massachusetts and earned his PhD at Georgetown in Genetics. While in graduate school, Ronald's wife worked at the NIH with a neurosurgeon, removing brain tumors. She would culture tumor cells and treat them with individual chemotherapies. At the time of her research, in the early 1980s, these were the only treatments available. The research objective was to see if there was a therapy that worked better for one patient over the other.

Her work was frustrating: "It often took weeks or months to get the process up. A lot of the time it was getting to the point where you could get results, and then the neurosurgeon would come in and say you can throw the cells away from patient number nine—they've passed away."

After completing post-doctorates at the University of Toronto and Case Western, Ronald took a job in 1986 at a biotech firm at a time when gene cloning was a new technology. "I was trained to do a lot of gene cloning," said Ronald. "After working for a few biotech companies on the scientific side, I realized I had an affinity for the business." In 2000, Ronald got a position with Bristol Myers Squibb to evaluate opportunities that came into the company from universities and companies and identify their potential at BMS. New opportunities ranged from oncology applications to software applications modeling proteins. Ronald met with professors doing some of the most cutting-edge research at universities, and some of the most promising emerging biotech firms. His affinity for business and realizing opportunities continued to develop. He identified Medarex as a company with the potential to use its technologies for making human antibodies. Their first product was targeting *CTLA4*, which was a way to interfere with immune system shutdowns.

"One of the things that happens in cancer is that your body shuts down the immune reaction. When this happens, your body can't destroy the cancer. This was a way to adjust that so that you didn't shut down inappropriately." Ronald saw this approach to cancer as a step ahead of the traditional potions. "At Medarex, we were fortunate that our first product program was very successful, and we partnered with BMS. When they saw the results in the phase 3 trial, they bought us."

Their product was based on work done by Dr. Jim Allison, awarded the Nobel Prize for his approach to cancer. Like Ronald, Allison saw the potential of harnessing the body's immune system to attack tumors rather than relying on poisonous cancer therapies. Allison had the insight to block a protein on T-cells that acts as a brake on their activation, freeing the T-cells to attack cancer. He developed an antibody to block the checkpoint protein *CTLA-4* and demonstrated the success of the approach in experimental models. His work led to the development of the first immune checkpoint inhibitor drug: Ipilimumab.[203]

Known commercially as Yervoy, now a Bristol Myers Squibb product, it became the first to extend the survival of patients with late-stage melanoma. Follow-up studies show 20 percent of those treated live for at least three years, with many living for ten years and beyond—unprecedented results. Subsequent research has extended this approach to new immune regulatory targets, most prominently PD-1 and PD-L1, with drugs approved to treat certain types and stages of melanoma, lung, kidney, bladder, gastric, liver, cervical, colorectal, and head and neck cancers and Hodgkin's lymphoma.[204]

In 1994 and 1995, Allison studied a known protein that functions as a brake on the immune system. He realized the potential of releasing the brake and thereby unleashing our immune cells to attack tumors. Allison had that antibody put into mice and saw their tumors shrink. His work ended up the hands of Medarex after being licensed out. Medarex was intrigued by this alternative way to treat patients and started the process of developing the drug. They talked to Bristol Myers Squibb, who had a very expensive patent on *CTL4* that Medarex knew they would need access to. They weren't interested initially in 1989 and 1990. So, Medarex continued to research and began manufacturing the antibody, putting it into a clinical trial.

203 "MD Anderson Immunologist Jim Allison Awarded Nobel Prize." 2020. MD Anderson Cancer Center.

204 Ibid.

In the phase one test, you really want to show that based on animal experiments, you have a safe drug. In this case, the drug showed its safety, then produced extremely positive results with a patient in San Diego who had a diagnosis for melanoma. The drug cured her cancer.

Medarex thought their success was unreal. Ronald, head of business development at the time, looked to find a partner for their drug, as it was expensive and risky. He talked to large and middle-sized pharmaceutical firms without generating interest. They didn't believe the therapy would work. "I banged on doors for a long time and nobody gave me the time of day. BMS listened but wasn't yet convinced. I courted them for four years before signing a deal," said Ronald.

Medarex developed the PD1 product that BMS now develops. It wasn't until the approval of Yervoy, Medarex's PD1, that people realized it actually worked. The pendulum began swinging to the other side after the Yervoy rollout. Now, many large drug manufacturers are eager to invest in similar therapies in immune oncology.

"Cancer patients successfully treated with immune checkpoint blockade are living proof of the power of basic science, of following our urge to learn and to understand how things work," said Allison.[205] Now, the trick is getting these drugs to work for more people.

One of today's challenges is that clinical success has outpaced our scientific knowledge of how these drugs work and how

---

205 Ibid.

they might best be combined with other therapies to improve treatment and reduce unwanted side effects. "We need more basic science research to do that," said Jim Allison.

So Allison and Ronald were at the forefront of immune oncology and treating cancer patients with antibodies that are less toxic to the body than some of the other treatments used to treat cancer. Yervoy became a huge blockbuster drug for Bristol Myers Squibb, which bought out Medarex to get their technology. "It went from being a shunned technology to something everyone wanted in a matter of years," said Ronald. "It was satisfying to be part of a new paradigm for a way that cancer would be treated."

One of the technologies Ronald helped release at Medarex was a product targeting dendritic cells that process foreign bodies that enter the human body. Ronald later had the opportunity to join Celldex. "Immunotherapy is our basis at Celldex—we are identifying ways of improving the immune reaction in patients," said Ronald. PD1 foreign antibodies, called check inhibitors, allow the immune reaction to continue in a patient. "It's like winning the lottery. If you have the right immune cells in your body that are going after the cancer and you get one of these checkpoint inhibitors, you have a good chance of getting a long-term cure."

The problem that still exists is that only a small portion of patients—around 15 to 20 percent—have the right immune cells to show significant positive and curing responses to these treatments. It's a time-intensive process to figure out what the right treatment is for each cancer patient. "So, what we're trying to do is condition the immune system by giving it the right antigens to go after the right tumor cells—that's our approach to immune oncology," said Ronald.

Trying to find a customized therapy in something as lethal as cancer can be very challenging with time constraints. While the cost of sequencing a patient's tumors has come down, it nevertheless still takes time. Today, Ronald and many other scientists are trying to figure out other ways to approach this time-to-treatment barrier.

Celldex now has components that can be added to the patients' immune system to stimulate their immune reaction. Sometimes this is delivered to the patient after they've been given a dose of radiation. The goal in radiation therapy is to hit the tumor and kill the cancerous cells. When the cells die, the contents of the cell are released. The contents of the tumor cells after being destroyed can be used to direct the immune response in the patient. The hope is to get material that has been released to the immune cells that are directing the immune response and can give them growth factors that will increase those numbers of cells and other factors that will help develop those cells. By giving a patient traditional cancer treatment with these additional factors, you may be able to enhance the immune system and destroy the cancer. Ronald and his colleagues are trying approaches similar to this: somewhat individualized, but not so individual that you couldn't do approach patients in the same way.

Another barrier in customizing cancer therapies for each patient is, of course, expense.

The company Dendreon, for example, would treat prostate cancer cells by sequencing the cancer cells and creating a vaccine tailored to the patient's individual needs. While their approach had reasonable success, cost was a major barrier. Their cost of the treatment itself was expensive, and the way it was reimbursed became a problem. "When prescribing the treatment, clinicians didn't want to put up $150,000 or more to get reimbursed at a later time," said Ronald. "They were expecting payment upfront, which is difficult for the payers and the patient. It became a nightmare from a logistics point of view to getting tumors cultured and then paying for treatment." Dendreon's approach was ultimately not successful, but their mission was no small feat.

The price for a PD1 inhibitor treatment, for example, can be $200,000. If Celldex develops another treatment that is less costly, how much will the system be able to absorb from what is still a very expensive treatment? One component of treatment may be $200,000 and owned by one company, and another component of the treatment may cost $100,000 owned by another company. Using these two components for the best possible outcome with such high price tags burdens the healthcare system.

Several companies are trying to control multiple treatment components offered to patients to better manage the pricing complexities of such expensive components and combinations. Celldex is trying to own a number of treatment components that can be controlled internally. Consequently, they're in a position to charge $150,000 to $200,000 but with all the pieces you would need, not just some of the pieces, for successful treatment. This process of multiple component development and ownership is very expensive for a smaller company to develop.

When examining cancer treatments, you're looking at an increased lifespan in terms of months, usually from three to nine months. While an incremental addition, it's important to the patient. Getting an extra nine months is immeasurable in value, but insurers don't like the high price tag, so many of these drugs are not reimbursed in Europe or the U.S. However, according to Ronald, the immune oncology drugs with potential for a long-term survival have a greater acceptance among patients for higher pricing.

Traditionally, the ratio of success to failure when developing a new cancer drug in the pharmaceutical industry is about one in ten. The hope is that you can find out early if it doesn't work before the third clinical trial to avoid spending on a product that may be safe but is ineffective. Phase three trials require the largest patient groups. It can be very expensive to treat and test each patient.

Ronald estimates that in cancer and oncology, the success rate is closer to one in twenty or in twenty-five. In some of the older approaches to chemotherapies, the toxicity is immediately obvious. With a lot of the new technologies, like recombinant antibodies, some of the antibodies are well tolerated by patients. "Unless these therapies have a severe toxicity in the patient, which has only been seen in one or two cases in thousands conducted, a new therapy may make it through the phase two trial, and may be safe but deceptively ineffective later on," said Ronald.

The consequence may be good science, but we still don't know how animal models are going to translate into human beings. It's difficult to determine what a new drug will look like in humans, even if it treats animals well. Science has cured many mice, but that doesn't necessarily help many patients directly.

CONCLUSION

"Whenever a treatment can extend the patient's life, it's tremendous, and whatever you can cure the patient, it's very satisfying," said Ronald. The gene therapy approaches are the main drive in oncology research because it has expanded the scope into CAR T-cells and engineered T cells and antigen receptor T-cells where companies are now showing (in mainly liquid tumors, blood cancers, leukemia, lymphomas) high percentages of patients have some sort of response.

Ronald thinks that in the future various combinations of these drugs are ultimately going to be successful. This will help us understand the mechanisms of the immune system and drive cancer research for the next ten or so years. All this progress is driving us toward more precise, targeted, effective treatments and potentially better patient outcomes.

CHAPTER 12:

INNOVATION IN CANCER TREATMENTS: BIG PHARMA TO BIOTECH

"Evolution selects those organisms that have been able to create major functions capable of coping with a future that is always unpredictable."

—ANTOINE DANCHIN

INNOVATION IN PHARMA

Ronald noted that the pharmaceuticals industry has evolved—most of the innovation, he says, is coming from small companies. Small companies are more willing to take a risk and try new approaches to developing drugs and experimenting with new treatments. When a treatment or product becomes successful, the large companies with significant capital reserves purchase these smaller companies and focus on market delivery, large-scale manufacturing, and commercialization of the products. For large biopharma companies, acquiring innovation is a cost-effective strategy.

At this junction, some researchers describe the relationships between large pharmaceutical firms and biotech start-ups as symbiotic—a sizeable number of venture capital investors that seed these small companies are hoping for quick success and returns from a timely buyout from larger companies. Many of the new, precise, targeted gene therapy, immuno-therapy, and other innovative treatments coming through are the products of smaller biotech firms and universities.

The pharmaceutical industry, like the tech industry described in *The Innovator's Dilemma*, has become a machine that develops drugs at a premium but is less involved with early stage research and development. Large pharmaceutical firms instead focus on late stage development and commercialization of new products to bring to market. The creation and research phases happen more often in smaller start-ups, later purchased by these larger machines.

Global pharmaceutical giants don't make the bulk of their revenue in research and development—that's the work of startups. As we explored in chapter 4, a McKinsey study on mergers and acquisitions in the pharmaceutical industry found that new drug development requires significant early stage investment for a generally low probability of success.[206] Late stage trials, however, also require high investment as well as the ability, expertise, and personnel to

---

206 "What's Behind The Pharmaceutical Sector's M&A Push." 2020. McKinsey & Company.

navigate regulatory pathways, which large pharmaceutical firms are more equipped to do. As a result, smaller, creative companies end up funding much of the innovation in early stage development. Once their research reaches advancement, large pharmaceutical firms—looking for the next "'alpha"— put up the reserves required to fund the expensive late stage trials and commercial marketing campaigns to roll out a new drug across the globe. Some say that commercialization is Merck's specialty within the pharmaceutical industry. Rob Burke is an example of a scientist who has worked in and out of the intuitional worlds of academia and big pharma to become an entrepreneur, developing the drugs he believes are the future of many medicines.

THE TYPICAL PHD ROUTE AND THE ATYPICAL ROB BURKE

Rob Burke holds a PhD in bioengineering and is a director at Avidity Biosciences. As an innovator, he shares the philosophy described in *The Innovator's Dilemma*. As an undergrad, Rob took an interest in nucleic acids. Many of Rob's friends in the bioengineering PhD world went into academia to continue researching and teaching. Rob, however, had a different intuition about the future of biopharma and precision medicine. He followed the excitement of gene therapy. He wanted to build a career in developing drugs that he thought had the most potential—the building blocks of protein, or nucleic acids. "Both DNA and RNA are nucleic acids, and therapeutics can be developed to mimic, augment, interfere with, control, replace, or edit nucleic acids. Nucleic acids will be at the forefront of therapeutic drug development to come for the next ten to fifteen years," said Rob.

Rob saw the potential of applying engineering principles to building better drugs and therapeutics. "What I thought would be the next ten to twenty years of drug development work that was about to be created was nucleic acid-based therapy. These therapies can be applied to patient treatments in many ways, as we are discovering and exploring."

Rob started his career at Merck & Co., where he fine-tuned drug development as a research scientist while continuing his undergraduate and graduate focus on nucleic acids. This was a training ground for Rob to learn the process of drug development. "It's a long, arduous slog to go from something that is a brand-new idea, to something that is an approved medicine that doctors can prescribe that will have a positive impact on human health," said Rob. "It takes on average ten to fifteen years and billions of dollars to make this happen."

Rob has seen mostly failure for new drug products and says the success rate is 10 percent, with a typical development period of ten to fifteen years. And yet, Rob has stuck with it. After five years with Merck, Rob left big pharma to work on his own vision. He wanted to work more with leanness and agility at Avidity Biosciences.

Rob's main competitor, siRNA Therapeutics, started development in 2001 and, thus, has the advantage of being first to market. When the opportunity came, Rob joined a startup company, Avidity Biosciences, and continued his wok in nucleic acid therapeutics, developing Antibody-siRNA Conjugates (ASCs) as a new class of drug candidates. ASCs utilizes the best features of both antibody-drug conjugates and nucleic acid-based medicines to create a transformational approach to the treatment of genetically defined diseases.

Precision medicine can mean almost anything in terms of going after a nucleic acid-based therapy. The degree depends on the precision. When picking a disease to treat, you have to look at underlying genetic drivers. Some will be relatively simple in terms of their mechanisms. For example, a mono-genetic disorder has one defined gene that might drive the formation of that disease. If you can target that one gene, you can treat or ameliorate the symptoms of the disease. Precision medicine, however, hopes to target a very specific gene with a very specific sequence with nucleic acid.

Gene therapy would be providing that specific gene. To treat genetic diseases driven by the lack of a functional copy of a gene, a gene therapy approach would be to provide that functional gene by delivering DNA or RNA (usually with a viral vector) into the cells that need to express the gene. To treat genetic diseases driven by the overexpression of a gene, a therapeutic approach would be to deliver small interfering RNA (siRNA) into the correct cells to reduce the expression of that gene.

TWO CASE STUDIES FOR GENE THERAPY AND SIRNA

Gene therapy: AveXis is a company that created a drug called ZOLGENSMA for patients with Spinal Muscular Atrophy (SMA), which replaces the function of the missing or non-working survival motor neuron 1 (SMN1) gene with a new, working copy of a human SMN gene that helps motor neuron cells work properly. This is again an example of innovation being purchased by a larger company. AveXis was acquired by Novartis for $8.7 billion in 2018.[207]

siRNA: Alnylam is a company that created a drug called inclisiran for patients with high LDL cholesterol levels, which reduces the expression of PCSK9 and promotes greater uptake of LDL out of the blood. Alnylam licensed the rights of its intellectual property, which was just acquired in a deal through a $9.7 billion deal with Novartis in November 2019.

HOW THIS APPLIES TO CANCER

Revisiting our earlier explanation of cancer, a cancer diagnosis is linked to cell mutations. In most cancers, it's not just one gene that has a mutation. The general consensus is the number of significant mutations—at least six in important pathways—is the threshold before it can be classified cancer. Tumors have to develop a way of avoiding detection to survive and grow within the body. The human body has its own defense mechanism to avoid mutations; this is a process called apoptosis wherein cells are programmed to kill themselves if mistakes during replication are made. In addition to apoptosis (programmed cell death), the body also uses its own immune system to fight cancer. In order to survive, cancer cells must evolve in a way to avoid immune surveillance so they are not destroyed by immune cells.[208]

---

207 "Novartis Enters Agreement To Acquire Avexis Inc. For USD 8.7 Bn To Transform Care In SMA And Expand Position As A Gene Therapy And Neuroscience Leader | Novartis." 2020. Novartis.

208 "Apoptosis: A Target For Anticancer Therapy." 2018. International Journal Of Molecular Sciences 19 (2): 448. doi:10.3390/ijms19020448.

A PRECISE AND INNOVATIVE APPROACH TO CAR T-CELL THERAPY

Effective CAR T-cell therapy starts with a genetic understanding of the cancer's mechanism.

This leads to a series of steps in drug development, such as:

- **Target identification and validation**: Identify the genetic driver as the cause of the disease.
- **Lead identification:** Find a compound that can modulate that gene to prevent or treat the disease.
- **Developing the lead:** Optimize and develop the lead and push it into clinical testing.

The challenge in this precision medicine approach is, again, identifying a way to make it efficient and cost effective. Rob thinks the next step in this line of cancer therapies is to discover and develop a platform by which to efficiently do this so each patient treatment, while individualized, will start with a platform with additional parts "switched out" as necessary. Developing a platform from which to start patient treatment, and making it more specific to their cancer or other disease, will make the therapy more cost effective and efficient.

GROWTH SIGNALS

In order for cancer to begin growing, cancerous cells must avoid the detection of multiple genetic defects. When treating cancer, you have the challenge of targeting multiple genes at the same time. For example, take a mutation in driver oncogene. You have a drug that is targeted and can fit this gene and turn its expression off to treat the cancer. However, the tumor can evolve to use an alternate pathway to escape the treatment, and thus maintains its ability to survive. To treat effectively, you want to hit multiple oncogenes at the same time. This is how treatments become increasingly complex. You don't want to hit all oncogenes with your treatment but, instead, precisely hit multiple oncogenes simultaneously. Then add the additional dimension of human genetic complexity on top of this.

"KRAS and p53 are classic oncogenes commonly mutated in cancer. Maybe you have also heard of BRCA mutations in breast cancer, or the designation "triple negative" breast cancer, which involves another classic oncogene called HER2," said Rob. Keytruda, a Merck product, is what they call a "checkpoint inhibitor" since it interferes with immune cell signaling by blocking a molecule called PD-1. Blocking PD-1 increases immune recognition of cancer. Merck is currently running a huge number of clinical trials combining their PD-1 blocker with other types of cancer treatments to improve efficacy.[209] Remember our discussion with Ronald Peppin and Bristol Myers Squibb's production of Yervoy and OPDIVO®? This is a direct competitor.

Think of two patients with pancreatic cancer tumors. The doctor sequences the genes of the tumors and might find the mutations are wildly different despite both patients having the same diagnosis. Patient-by-patient differences make an efficient and standard treatment process very complex. At some level, you could think of building precision medicine as personalized medicine. You have to determine what each

---

209 "KEYTRUDA® (Pembrolizumab)." 2020. Keytruda.com.

patient's individual genetic makeup is, and then tailor your medicine with specific combinations of genetic defects for the individual patient.

In terms of drug development and the business case for how many patients can be treated, the cost of the drug will normally be spread across 100,000 patients, but each drug is individual and for just one patient. Every drug made with this approach is in some sense now personalized. The challenge for this realm of precision medicine is to build a platform or technology to switch out certain parts for patients, rather than building it from scratch each time. Rob and his team, as well as a host of other companies, are trying to do exactly this. "One challenge for personalized medicine is then how to diffuse the cost of development when there is only a single patient," said Rob.

Car T-cell therapies don't work for all patients, but according to Rob, 30 to 40 percent of patients, in some cases, have tumors that have been effectively removed with their own cells after being reprogrammed and simulating a natural immune response to cancerous cells that previously avoided detection. In some cases, the effects have been 10 percent or lower, however. This is a complex therapy, but Rob and his colleagues think it's the future of cancer treatment. He thinks the next generation of these therapies will be mass produced but also tailored. From a manufacturing standpoint, this is much more attractive because you can still treat patterns, and it's easier to develop.

A few case studies to note here to examine how this is developing in the industry:

- Juno (acquired by Celgene for $9 billion, and now Celgene acquired by Bristol Myers Squibb for $65 billion) and Kite (acquired by Gilead for $11.9 billion) built CAR-T therapies that require a patient's own cells to be taken out, altered, and then infused back in.[210]
- Allogene is a private company that has raised close to $1 billion in capital to develop allogeneic CAR-T therapy, where universal donor cells can be used for any patient—instead of requiring a patient's own cells. This will drastically improve the ease of manufacturing.[211]

The biotech industry is about innovation and pushing the envelope of what's possible. We are able to treat more diseases than anyone thought possible over the last century, but it isn't enough. It's why Rob and his colleagues all wake up and go to work every day. Rob thinks it may take five, ten, or even twenty years to build these platforms, but this is part of the excitement. In siRNA-based therapeutics, 2018 was a landmark year, having received its first FDA-approved therapy for a market treatment.

TIMELINE

- siRNA initially discovered in 1999.
- In 2000, more siRNA identified in plants and mammalian cells.

---

210 McGrane, Clare. 2018. "Juno Therapeutics Acquired By Celgene For $9B In Dramatic Deal For Rising Biotech Star." Geekwire.
211 "Allogeneic Cell Therapy | Allogene Therapeutics." 2020. Allogene

- siRNA Therapeutics company acquired by Merck in 2006.[212]
- Nearly fifteen years later, this company had their first drug approved.

This is a long time to go through countless experiments, but along the way, we've had glimmers of hope. Alnylam, for example, has a platform technology with a pipeline with their development of ONPATTRO®.[213] For them, this first approval was the beginning.[214] Rob anticipates that over the next ten years, a whole pipeline of siRNA drugs will be approved.

While Rob anticipates that we'll have treatment for all cancers in the next five years, it's also possible that there will be more and more varieties of cancer to tackle. "More and more platform technologies are coming online, and a lot of untranslatable diseases now have some treatment options. We have genetically defined medicines and can treat patients that have had no options before. It starts with a genetic understanding of the mechanism of the disease," said Rob.

Again, human genetics are exceptionally complex. No one knows the optimal diet for humans, and no one has done a clinical trial on this for humans, let alone what genetics will do for a certain patient. Rob thinks this is the next wave of diving into the details, which tech companies like Google are beginning to do.

---

212 "Merck & Co., Inc. Announces Completion of Acquisition of Sirna Therapeutics, Inc." Merck & Co. R.
213 "After Big Year, RNAi Drugmakers Compete To Prove What Comes Next." 2020. Biopharma Dive.
214 "Alion Pharmaceuticals – San Francisco, CA." 2020.

For years, doctors have treated melanoma patients. And for years, there wasn't much he could offer them. "Cancer always figures out a way to get around a drug that targeted a single pathway," Atkins said. But in the last couple of years, new developments in immunotherapy means he can expect more than half of his melanoma patients can be "cured" of their cancer.[215]

DAVID KODACK'S STORY

David works as an Investigator at Novartis studying cancer and developing cancer cell therapies with a precision medicine approach. After earning a doctorate, he moved to Boston and completed a post-doctoral research fellowship at Massachusetts General Hospital and Harvard Medical School. "My academic background and research at Georgetown served as a foundation for moving into the commercial and innovation space in Boston, where academia is applied in the start-up and commercial world." David's mind opened up to the entrepreneurial spirit of creating a company unique to Boston and different from D.C.

David collaborated with a number of different scientists working on their post-docs and hospitals on cancer patient research. His research facility is in close proximity to a cancer treatment center. Here, at David's clinic, the patient would be treated using genetics as one point to review in examining treatment options. One of David's collaborators was cultivating patient tumors once they became resistant to treatment.

---

215 "Georgetown Physician Leads National Melanoma Study." 2015. Medstar Georgetown University Hospital.

The roadblock many physicians and researchers faced was that once a patient's cancerous tumor stopped responding to treatments, there were no other therapies to offer. David and his team wanted to investigate why this roadblock existed. David and his team started to culture these tumors to better understand why they weren't responding to treatment. From this, they built a model based on genetic sequencing to understand how the tumor behaved and why it did or didn't react to certain treatments. "The main goal of cultivating cancer cells was that the genetics don't tell us everything (as far as how they respond to treatment. Genetics are a good place to start and we've successfully developed good therapies against them over the last twenty years, but there is more to it than that. Not all patients with the same genetics respond the same way," said David. "Therefore, other factors must play a role."

THE QUESTION

It became clear that there were genetic links to why some patients weren't responding to treatment, but other factors as well. David's team used this model to develop a question: could the cancer cells be used as a diagnostic by which to design a treatment for cancer? David and his team started comparing the responses of patients to their own treatments, retrospectively.

CURRENT STATE: THE PROCESS

The team's question and model led them to a more precise approach to treating cancer and a vision for what the future state could look like. They would first sample the cancerous tumor cells and sequence them. After sequencing, the team would expose the cancer cells to various cancer treatments to determine how the patient reacted to treatment retroactively. The drugs that the cancer cells best responded to could be prescribed to the patient. In several cases, patients showed the same response to the cancer drugs as the cancer cells had. In other cases, however, it was clear there were other factors besides genetics impacting responses to treatments. "It's a relatively simple idea, so it's surprising it hadn't been done yet," said David.

So, to summarize, currently the way the tumor biopsy incorporating sequencing works is:

- **Patient diagnosis**: The patient has pathology and next-generation sequencing tests (genetic test for the mutated genes).
- **Treatment decision**: On the basis of the test results, a treatment decision is made about how to treat the patient's tumor.

One challenge with this approach is the amount of time the testing and diagnosis takes, as well as decisions about how to proceed with treatment options. With a quickly spreading cancer, time to effective treatment is very significant for better outcomes.

FUTURE STATE

In the future, many agree some of this timing in diagnosis and treatment can be reduced. The future state would look something like this:

- **Diagnosis**: The patient would undergo a short-term culture and drug screen to identify the cancer while determining the best treatment option.
- **Treatment decision**: A better match for the patient could be quickly identified to provide better outcomes. [216]

INDUSTRY ADOPTION OF THIS PRECISE APPROACH

The scientific world is still working to perfect this approach, but there are a number of emerging techniques to culture patient's cancer cells before prescribing treatment. Whether this is fast enough to be able to design a therapy is unknown. With David's research team, the turnaround time on average was slow for each patient. David himself admits that this isn't an efficient business model. The approach to treating a patient's cancer by the genetics of the cancer, however, is growing and has for the last twenty years, and it is a good starting point.

There are clinical trials now being run in leukemia where patient's cells are taken from their blood, cultured short-term, and then exposed to a handful of drugs. Based on the cells' responses to the drug, one is chosen to move forward. Of course, there are many complexities that this approach doesn't always address and doesn't always make it successful. There is the issue of cancer tumor heterogeneity—the idea that the cancer's cells aren't homogenous, or identical, but differ from one another in genetic makeup and mutation from the original, healthy cell.

---

216 Kodack et al. "Primary Patient Derived Cancer Cells and their Potential for Personalized Cancer Patient Care."

Cancer is a dynamic disease. Throughout its progression, cancer generally becomes more heterogeneous. "As a result of this heterogeneity, the bulk tumor might include a diverse collection of cells that have distinct molecular signatures with differential levels of sensitivity to treatment."[217]

This heterogeneity may result in genetic variations within cancer cells in the same tumor, which creates sub-populations with genetic distinctions from one another. This variation and heterogeneity between cancer cells enable drug resistance. Some cancerous cells may respond to a drug, and other cancerous cells within the same tumor, with genetic variation between one another, may continue growing and multiplying. Some of these cells may be unaffected by the treatment. The effects of this during treatment my mean that some of the cancerous cells will respond to treatment, and some cells won't respond, hence, like in Francois's case, the application of multiple therapies. This highlights the importance of a "precision" approach to effective cancer treatments; an accurate assessment of tumor heterogeneity is essential for the development of effective therapies.

Novartis is able to do this in its Car T-cell therapies—leukemia, CLL CART primary antigen receptor have been FDA approved. In a CAR T cell therapy, a patient's cells are engineered to attack a receptor on the cancer cell. Response rates in this approach have been remarkable. This

217 Dagogo-Jack, Ibiayi, and Alice T. Shaw. 2017. "Tumour Heterogeneity And Resistance To Cancer Therapies." Nature Reviews Clinical Oncology 15 (2): 81-94.

can, however, sometimes cause an autoimmune response where the patient's cells begin attacking normal, healthy cells. Currently, the RNA immunotherapy approach is capital – and time-intensive. This approach takes slightly more than two weeks per patient. However, researchers are working to reduce this evaluation to a much shorter time frame to make it a scalable and efficient approach to treating more patients.

In David's career he has seen, and envisions, the following in precision medicine:

1. A wave of identifying/sequencing all the mutations associated with cancerous cells.
2. Learning how to target those mutations precisely.
3. Targeting the protein related to transcription factors that wire and control a number of different biological processes. Here, you have to target protein-to-protein interactions at the molecular level. David acknowledges that this will be the more challenging step.

David thinks identifying and understanding these new protein targets isn't the only means through which to review, evaluate, and eventually treat cancer patients. To him, it's also important to review the tumor's micro-environment. Being able to mimic this micro-environment will provide more understanding for effective treatment, like the environment of the human body the tumor may grow in. Growing a cancer cell in a plastic Petri dish as opposed to its growth in the human body is important to consider. These are very different environments for cells to grow in and, thus, produce different behaviors and responses. There are groups doing more 3D matrix assays now to understand this. "We are learning more about how to recapitulate the end zero tumor," said David. David thinks more targeted therapies will result from this work, this emerging body of knowledge, and these developments. Now, most tumors are sequenced, so there are frequencies within mutations that have been identified.

NOTORIOUSLY MUTATED GENES

A mutagen is an agent, like a chemical or radiation, that causes a genetic mutation. Certain genes are notorious for mutating and causing or linking to cancer. And there are specific mutagens known for causing base mutations in the DNA, such as UV light and smoking, which cause a different mutation. David thinks you can map genes based on the lineage and status to determine what could cause the mutation.

DAVID'S LONG-TERM VIEW

Some of the mutations we have don't necessarily lead to cancer. Thus, having early detection mechanisms and diagnostics would be great, and monitoring patients in how they're responding in a more dynamic way rather than just scanning and imaging the cancer repeatedly may lead to better outcomes, said David.

CONCLUSION

So, whether it's Rob at Merck, David at Novartis, or Ronald at Bristol Myers Squib, big and small firms around the world are working to better understand cancer in more precise ways. Smaller firms may have more agility to be innovative with research, later selling their work to large pharmaceutical firms to market and commercialize. Large pharma firms are investing heavily in immune oncology and CAR T-cell therapies. Billions are being invested annually around the world to better understand and treat cancer in more targeted, precise ways. No one has the answer, but new ideas are emerging quickly—like Rob's, David's, and Ronald's—that are more precise and targeted in their approach, using data points along the way to inform and guide research. Bristol Myers Squibb has created an entirely new division of its firm, Business Insights and Intelligence, to use data points along the way of every executive decision to become nimbler and more innovative, identifying it as instrumental in its transition from a pharmaceutical firm to a biopharmaceutical firm positioned for growth.

No two cancers are the same, and early detection is key. The more we understand about the genome—what genes are responsible for, molecular-level interactions between proteins, and how the environment of a cancer may affect its growth—the better we will be at diagnosing, treating, and maybe even curing cancer. This will require a global and collaborative approach to building and testing ideas, partnerships between different types of firms, and significant investments of time, money, research, and patience. While we may never totally cure cancer for every patient, we have to try. Thankfully, our biopharma future that has more data and information to work with than ever before.

While advances in sequencing technology and target identification have had a major impact, only a small fraction of cancer patients is treated based on the identification of specific genetic mutations. Much remains to be learned. [218]

---

218 Kodak, et al. "Primary Patient Derived Cancer Cells and their potential for Personalized Cancer Patient Care." Massachusetts General Hospital Cancer Center.

CHAPTER 13:

THE BIOTECH REVOLUTION IN CHINA

"The rapid rise of China's nascent biomedicine capability shows how policy support and regulatory reform can transform an industry and rally the capital necessary to grow it."[219]

—UBS CHIEF INVESTMENT OFFICE

THE BIOTECH REVOLUTION IS GLOBAL

Biotech companies, academic research institutions, software companies, analytics, data management companies, scientists, researchers, doctors, and readers like yourself are driving the precision medicine movement forward. This isn't a national revolution but a global one. Countries like China, Australia, and India are investing in precision medicine movements and progress is ongoing.[220]

---

219 "China's Biotech Revolution." 2020. Chief Investment Office.

220 Markets, Research. 2020. "Global Strategic Evaluation Of Precision Medicine Markets 2016-2026 & Country Analysis For Emerging Opportunities."

Advances in biotechnology, genetics, and biopharmaceuticals are obviously not exclusive to the United States and western Europe. In China, the Beijing Genomics Institute (BGI) has become the world's largest genomics organization.[221] BGI was established in 1999, originally founded as a completely state-run enterprise at Beijing University. BGI participated in the Human Genome Project in its infancy and contributed to less than 1 percent of the project's findings. Within a decade, however, BGI quickly grew to become an organization invested in research and development in genomics around the world, with several large initiatives behind it.

According to some measures, the Beijing Genomics Institute, in addition to being the world's largest genomics organization, has the world's largest genome sequencing center.[222] One division of BGI is listed on the Shenzhen Stock Exchange and is a semi-commercial non-profit endeavor.[223] Seeing the potential applications of genetics in agriculture, human health, and business, BGI has combined the three advances discussed in the book's opening into one large organization to drive national efforts such as Healthy China 2020—an effort to provide universal health care treatment to everyone in China by 2020.[224]

---

221 "BGI Is A Global Genomics Organization – We Provide Fast, Accurate, Affordable Genomic Data For All Your Sequencing Needs." 2020. BGI – Global.

222 "Can China Become A Scientific Superpower?" 2019. The Economist.

223 "BGI Genomics Announces Pricing Of Initial Public Offering – BGI – US." 2017. BGI – US.

224 "The Pursuit Of Healthy China 2020 | Asia Outlook Magazine." 2020. Asia Outlook Magazine.

The Chinese government looks at investing in health initiatives that benefit its population as an investment in its workforce and its future, argues KPMG Chairman Mark Britnell. "There's an increasing appreciation across the world now that decent healthcare is essential to economic growth; and spending on it should be seen as an investment in future growth, not a cost. Work by KPMG found that for every year of life expectancy increases, GDP increases by 4 percent in the long run. So, wealth and health are inextricably linked."[225]

BGI conducts CRISPR research, develops genome sequencers, compiles and analyzes genomics data, and tries to combine all these research findings directly to clinical care, agriculture, and other industries. Their genomics footprint and mission appear to be broader than any single business in the genomics space in the U.S. It isn't just building sequencers, understanding and perfecting CRISPR gene therapies and CAR T-cell therapies, or analyzing genomics data with AI. Unlike U.S. and western European companies, BGI takes on all of these aspects in one business heavily subsidized by the Chinese government.

There is no question BGI is making progress in many realms within genetics. BGI had twice as many agriculture publications in *Nature* and *Science* than the U.S. last year. In China, there are fewer data privacy concerns and regulatory hurdles to jump through in conducting CRISPR research on humans. Many people I spoke with over the course of writing this book were opposed to having their genome sequenced at all, and feared that companies could use the data against

---

225 Ibid.

them—employers may one day use it as a means of discrimination, and searches for genes such as the "gay gene" could be used to eradicate certain segments of the population in the future.

According to their website, Omics for All, BGI's self-identified mission is to "use genomics to benefit mankind, and to be a leader in the era of life sciences."[226] Whether or not the U.S. government and Chinese government agree about the use of genomics data, China seems to be making progress on the genetics frontier. "China definitely has the foundation to contribute and make discoveries on those frontiers, particularly now that such a big investment has been made," says Daniel Voytas, a plant geneticist at the University of Minnesota in St. Paul who invented an early genome-editing system before later adopting CRISPR. An example of immediate applications in genetics to a pressing public concern and need are applying sequencing technology to the coronavirus to better understand how it works and how it can be treated.

BGI began as an academic division of Beijing University and was mostly operated by the Chinese government.[227] Wanting to operate more like a business, BGI announced its entrance on the Shenzhen Stock Exchange to become a publicly traded company and began opening up its research projects and partnerships globally. Twenty years after their inception, BGI has research partnerships, projects, and offices in over a hundred regions and countries around the world.

---

226 "BGI Group Official Website." 2020. En.Genomics.Cn.
227 Cohen, Jon. 2019. "Fields Of Dreams." Science 365 (6452): 422-425. doi:10.1126/science.365.6452.422.

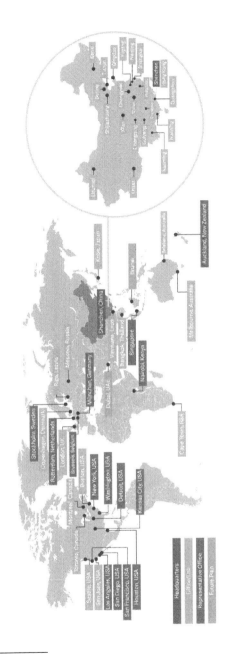

228

228 "Regions-BGI Group Official Website." 2020. En.Genomics.Cn.

Interest in genomics in the Pacific region has spread to countries outside of China. In 2018, Australia announced a government-led initiative to invest $500 million into genomics over the next decade for its human genome project. In 2018, it was estimated that $4.2 billion was invested in private biotech start-ups in the U.S. from Asian investors.[229] China also recently announced its Precision Medicine Initiative to improve the quality and precision of healthcare for its citizens.

BGI is actively involved in this in the China National GeneBank Project. Overall, the project is an ambitious undertaking with the self-advertised mission of making genetic resources "Owned by All, Completed by All, and Shared by All."[230] With a population exceeding 1.4 billion, China has an enormous group from which to pull genomics data.[231] Since genes are the language and basis for all living creatures on earth, we can learn an enormous amount about how all this information is connected and related by comparing genomics data. One of the China National GeneBank's ideas is that by creating a repository for all this genetic information, we can, to some degree, help ensure that certain species or genes are propagated in the future.

Part of BGI's, and more broadly, China's interest in genetics and biotechnology is establishing ways to feed its massive

---

229 "Top 10 Asia Biopharma Clusters 2018." 2018. GEN – Genetic Engineering And Biotechnology News.

230 "China National GeneBank-BGI Group Official Website." 2020. En. Genomics.Cn.

231 "To Feed Its 1.4 Billion, China Bets Big On Genome Editing Of Crops." 2019. Science | AAAS.

population. Genomics data from food combined CRISPR to edit crop genes and create new crop varieties can help feed the world's largest population. A significant portion of the China National GeneBank thus focuses on agricultural work in genomics.

"Massive genomic data is generated by large-scale research projects. Therefore, it is imperative to build a public data platform which is capable to collect, store, and manage data to support data exploration, utilization, and sharing," writes the GeneBank.[232]

Their website also offers data visualization tools to compare, analyze, and understand genomics data currently under development. Their developing phylogenetic tree tool will show evolutionary branches of different life forms from fish to trees to humans, and which organisms are descended from and related to others—tracing, in theory, back to a singular point of common origin, as theorized by Charles Darwin. Their map visualization tool, also under development, hopes to show the geographies of genomics distribution between humans around the world. Their human chromosome map, again under development, aims to show distributions of human genomics data at different chromosomal locations and variation distribution for chromosomal locations.

Another division of the China National GeneBank is a Bioinformatics Center, which is working to develop a public

---

232 "China National GeneBank-BGI Group Official Website." 2020. En. Genomics.Cn.

data platform that would have the capability to collect, store, and analyze genomics data to allow researchers and individuals to utilize, share, and explore what it all means. The Bioinformatics Center has created thirteen databases of genomics data for plants, insects, birds, microorganisms, DNA profiles, diseases, and more.

Like a Google search, in the genetic disease database, you type in the name of a gene into a search bar. The database populates results for the gene, its variants, associated diseases, and genes associated with the phenotype. Think what this database could eventually show—the gene family, information about not only how the gene operates individually but also how it operates collectively, what other species the gene is found in, and its ultimate origins. What it also reveals is how diseases can behave differently in organisms with the same genetic makeup.

According to Dr. Robert Klitzman, a director of clinical psychiatry at Columbia University and author of *Am I My Genes?*, humans share 99.9 percent of the same genetic makeup between individuals. So, between you and me, that's a 0.1 percent difference. Much of this genetic data is shared with other organisms.[233] This then raises the question that Dr. Klitzman raises—are we our genes and is our health predetermined? The answer is that our genetics certainly doesn't determine everything.

After yielding search results on a gene with its variants, a list of diseases associated with it, and what the gene may

---

233 Klitzman, Robert. 2012. *Am I My Genes?*

mean, there is a clinical management tool listing what treatments have helped patients in the past manage their disease that had the gene after undergoing a genetic test. In this case, it seems that an understanding of our genetic makeup can reveal helpful information about how to treat diseases through what worked for other patients with the same genetic mutation.

Another section after searching for a gene is in what animals it can be found. For example, after searching for the gene and locus *POU3F4*, which lists its location in patients with deafness, it also includes information on mice that have carried the gene and showed similar cases of deafness.[234] Check it out for yourself and discover what some of your own genes may mean.

Here's a visual diagram, both linear and radial, of the *POU3F4* gene:

234 "GDRD: Genetic Disease And Rare Disease Database – Cngbdb." 2020. Db.Cngb.org.

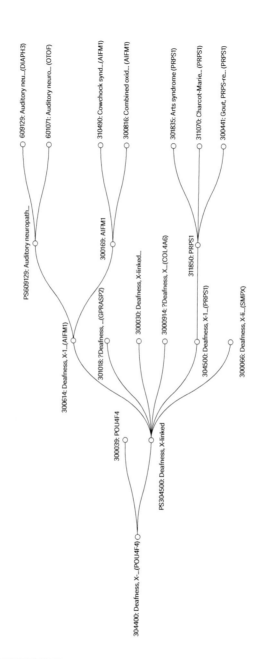

235 "OMIM – Online Mendelian Inheritance In Man." 2020. Omim.org.

So think about all the applications of this data becoming available to global citizens all over the world. What does it mean to you to uncover your genetic makeup, and what would you use it for? For me, the journey to uncover my genes and understand what they mean began with my Stargardt's diagnosis. What began with a visit to the doctor's office resulted in my medical diagnosis as a disabled person. While the legal definition of this disability helps in getting a larger monitor at work or extra time on an examination, I'd never refer to myself as disabled. While my low vision is based in genetics, it isn't currently my genetic makeup that gives me the legal term disabled: it's the physical result of this genetic mutation and other environmental factors, that does. Two of Stargardt's patients of the same age may often very different visual acuity, for example.

So let's think through what BGI could be doing with all this genetic data and what the China National GeneBank could be, too. Is it a Noah's Ark: a collection of different blueprints of humans, flora, and fauna within the borders of China that may one day be extinct but are now preserved in a database?

According to *Asia Times*, the China National GeneBank was only established in 2018, but now has a collection of over twenty million genomes.[236] The hope, according to the same source, is to scale the collection to over three hundred million samples in their second stage of development. Similar gene bank projects exist in the States (the U.S. Center for Biotechnology and Information), the United Kingdom (The

---

236 2020. Asiatimes.com.

European Bioinformatics Institute), and Japan (DNA Data Bank of Japan).

Chinese spending on research and development in science increased tenfold from 2000 to 2016.[237] I was personally shocked in 2018 when the first-ever CRISPR gene-editing experiment was performed on a human embryo. The scientist behind the experiment, He Jiankui, has scientific and educational backgrounds in both Chinese and western education. He started his studies at the University of Science and Technology of China, then continued at Rice and Stanford Universities in the U.S. Ultimately, the Chinese government recruited him to return to China under its "Thousand Talents" program. In Shenzhen, He began his entrepreneurial project to gene edit a human embryo that would become an adult. He performed the experiment on what became two baby girls, which was internationally criticized as illegal and ethically unsound.[238]

This development pushed the boundaries of what many scientists in the world thought was reasonable and acceptable. It sparked conversations between scientists, newspapers, and on a personal level with many of my friends. The ultimate consensus is that we are far from fully understanding the implications of gene editing in human health. This is a brand-new technology and we only understand a small percentage of the human genome.

237 "Can China Become A Scientific Superpower?" 2019. The Economist.
238 Ibid.

Progress in genetics, however, is moving forward globally as we continue to learn and make new discoveries. China is publishing nearly 23 percent of the world's scientifically peer-reviewed papers on gene editing—a little more than half of what the U.S. is currently publishing.[239]

In 2017, a study was performed by Zuo Wei in Shanghai to improve lung tissue damage from pollution and smoking in patients using stem cells. Wei removed lung tissue from four patients. He then isolated the most healthy-looking stem cells from the sample, helped them multiply, and sprayed them back into the lungs of the patients. The procedure was reported to have improved the health of the lung tissue in two of the four patients.[240]

China's National GeneBank already holds the genomes of over 140,000 Chinese citizens.[241] When I interviewed Bradley Murray, the computational biologist, his impression was that CAR T-Cell therapies were outpacing advances made in the U.S. BGI, beyond extending globally, has also expanded its business and research capabilities through large acquisitions. In 2013, BGI acquired Complete Genomics in Mountainview, California, after competitor Illumina tried unsuccessfully to make the acquisition.[242] Then, BGI became the largest purchaser of Illumina's sequencing machines, purchasing over

---

239 Ibid.
240 Ibid.
241 Ibid.
242 "Can A Chinese Company's Powerful New Genome Sequencer Compete In The U.S.?" 2018. STAT.

130 of them, and China became Illumina's second-largest market after the U.S.[243]

BGI claims their newest sequencer, the MGISEC-T7, can now sequence a complete genome in twenty-four hours for $600 with a highly accurate and thorough analysis of a DNA, making it the cheapest in today's global market.[244] The capabilities of the MGISEC-T7 are comparable to one of Illumina's sequencers, the NovaSeq line. When it comes to sequencing, BGI wants to make it "affordable to everyone around the world, which isn't the mission of our competitors."[245] With Illumina's most cutting-edge machine, sequencing an entire genome with a highly accurate read will cost around $1,000. Since its sale of sequencers to BGI, Illumina has filed lawsuits against the company for its sequencing patents in the U.S., Denmark, Turkey, and Switzerland.[246]

Unlike public and private companies in the U.S. exploring the use of gene sequencing data with drug development, BGI is heavily subsidized by the Chinese government, which, in turn, impacts how they function. Illumina, for example only develops and sells gene sequencers and software tools to help researchers analyze the data. The information from the sequencers is what other, separate companies doing work in clinical applications like developing gene therapies. Illumina also has no ownership over the data it sequences. In China, all data sequenced by Illumina's machines and

---

243 "Can A Chinese Company's Powerful New Genome Sequencer Compete In The U.S.?" 2018. STAT.
244 Ibid.
245 Ibid.
246 Ibid.

stored on the cloud *isn't* shared with Illumina, and it's in this genomics data that the value lies. While the NIH has established the Human Genome Research Institute with a database of genomes, it isn't an open platform and accessible to the public like BGI's database is.

In the U.S. there are competing voices and visions about the best path forward for genomics and its use of data to develop treatments. In China, however, without a platform for public discussion and with one company compiling genomic data into a database across plants, animals, humans, and other living organisms, comes rapid scientific advancement. In the U.S., many researchers that have been conducting years of work on genomics data have no place to compile it, and no central repository for the whole country's genomics information. This isn't the case in China. And, in theory, the more genetic data we have compiled in one place to compare and analyze, the more quickly we can understand what it all means.

Data privacy concerns in the U.S. slow down the advances of genomics. Data privacy in the context of China, however, is considered differently. We are at this point where we have a lot of potential in China, where biotech is booming, according to Victor Li. But the ecosystem and platforms for innovation in China have tried to encourage companies to go public in Hong Kong. China is trying to learn from the US and create a similar biotech ecosystem, particularly with encouraging biotech companies to go public in Hong Kong. "Some of these biotechs are becoming profitable companies," said geneticist Victor Li.

CONCLUSION: SURROUNDING INVESTMENTS IN ASIA IN BIOTECH

In 2016, Asian investors funding in the venture capital biopharma space totaled only 11 percent of the investment. Biotechnology and pharmaceutical manufacturing are notorious for being capital intensive. It requires significant investment in infrastructure, advanced manufacturing technology, and equipment. It also needs a capital-abundant market to fund research and development, which often results in very expensive experiments with few promising results.

While much of this is still true, it is again no longer true that biopharmaceutical development and research happens exclusively in the U.S. and western Europe. We are seeing significant advances in the Asian market in biopharmaceutical companies, investment, research and development, infrastructure, pharmaceutical and cellular therapeutic manufacturing, and promising results.

In Jakarta, Indonesia, Kalbe Farma began constructing the country's first biopharmaceutical manufacturing plant in 2018. The plant will develop biological products and materials for cellular-based therapies, such as monoclonal antibodies. Kalbe Farma has also announced its intentions to allocate $14 million to transferring some of its research and development efforts from South Korea and China.[247]

Thailand recently announced its economic growth strategy for the next twenty years, titled Thailand 4.0.[248] Under its

247 Markets, Research. 2020. "Global Strategic Evaluation Of Precision Medicine Markets 2016-2026 & Country Analysis For Emerging Opportunities."
248 Ibid.

investment priorities fall biotechnology, biomed, health, and wellness. Tax exemptions are now offered in Thailand for biotechnology firms, with their intention to become a global medical hub by 2026. Thailand is developing a reputation, even among Americans, as being a destination for cheap, quality medical care.

The current prime minister of Malaysia, Abdullah Ahmad Badawi, announced a fifteen-year investment strategy in biotechnology in hopes of bringing it up to compose 5 percent of Malaysia's total GDP.[249]

In 2018, Merck announced plans to invest in a $15 million project in Singapore to construct the BioReliance laboratory, which will be Merck's first in the region.[250] Amgen has also opened a manufacturing support office in Singapore, at Tuas Biomedical Hub. Termed the "Next Gen Workplace," it was developed to raise Amgen's investments in Singapore to $291 million and inspire more innovation and collaboration within the firm. The number of biotech startups in Singapore has also skyrocketed from around twenty-five in 2007 to nearly fifty in 2018, according to the Agency for Science, Technology, and Research.[251]

The Department of Treasury has also expanded its oversight of foreign investment in biotechnology in the U.S. the Committee on Foreign Investment included "research and

---

249 Ibid.
250 Ibid.
251 Ibid.

development in biotechnology" under its twenty-seven "critical technology" industries subject to review.[252]

President Tsai Ing-wen of Taiwan announced his 5+2= 7 industries plan objective is to grow the economy by investing in five industry sectors, which includes biopharma. The biotech industry in Taiwan is estimated to have doubled in the last decade to $3.55 billion in 2016. The pharma industry there is now valued at $45.2 billion.[253] Part of Taiwan's plan to bolster its biopharma, biotech, and medical device industry and economy is to develop and market twenty new drugs by 2025 and establish at least ten new "flagship brand" biotech and health-related corporations, through organic growth or acquisitions.[254]

Australia has announced its plans to invest $335 million AUS over the next decade in its human genome project. They have also established an organization to promote the health, wellness, and citizen longevity by expanding access to genomics technology, information, and knowledge in its Australian Genomics Health Futures Mission.[255]

India too announced its plans to develop its first biotech-focused university in 2018. To date, the country has more than four hundred pharmaceutical companies, according to the Pharmaceutical Export Promotion Council. The India Brand

---

252 2020. Home.Treasury.gov. Program.
253 Markets, Research. 2020. "Global Strategic Evaluation Of Precision Medicine Markets 2016-2026 & Country Analysis For Emerging Opportunities."
254 Ibid.
255 Ibid.

Equity Foundation also lists approximately eight hundred biotech companies. [256]

What we can see is that investment in biotech around the world in unexpected places is growing and continuing, enabling us to learn more quickly and raising questions for how this technology should be responsibly used around the world.

---

256 Ibid.

CHAPTER 14:

CELLULAR THERAPIES OF THE FUTURE

"Life is creative in the strongest possible sense."

–ANTOINE DANCHIN

A GLIMPSE OF ASTRAZENECA

AstraZeneca is a global, science-led biopharmaceutical company that focuses on the discovery, development, and commercialization of prescription medicines. Their primary focus is developing treatments for diseases in oncology, cardiovascular, renal and metabolism, and respiratory. AstraZeneca operates in over one hundred countries, and its innovative medicines are used by millions of patients worldwide.[257] Unsurprisingly, oncology is a key growth driver for the company as it continues to expand its reach in a $100

---

257 "Astrazeneca – Research-Based Biopharmaceutical Company." 2020. Astrazeneca.com.

billion dollar plus global cancer market.[258] What's interesting is the shift in approach to developing treatments for diseases such as cancer; AstraZeneca is a prime example of a company that is scaling this shift in manufacturing.

VISITING A MANUFACTURING FACILITY

I walked through the winding corridors of a 650+ employee facility in Fredrick, Maryland. This $200 million-dollar annual operation is in the business of biopharmaceuticals. A friend of mine is an industrial engineer who has worked at the facility for several years. We clad ourselves in gowns, hairnets, booties, and are sanitized before entering the facility.

Sterile, white corridors are filled with brightly colored red, yellow, blue, and green tubes and pipes that wind throughout the facility. Each tube has a color-coding scheme that corresponds to sterility boundaries. Here, they grow what are becoming some of the building blocks for cancer treatments: proteins. At this facility, they are harvested from cells, formulated to proper concentration, and then distributed globally as large molecule medicines.

STANDARDIZING AN "UNSTANDARDIZED" PROCESS

These protein building blocks are what many researchers believe are the platform, foundation, and future for many cancer and rare disease therapies. At facilities like this one, they're making proteins in large stainless-steel bioreactors. From start to finish, the process takes around

---

258 Ibid.

fifty days from first vessel inoculation to final packaging. As a scientific company, AstraZeneca has gone through great lengths to build a robust process that is constantly monitored. Any deviation in the production process is extensively investigated. Years of meticulously tested and proven science and engineering have culminated in a level of standardization that has enabled this technology to be consistently safe enough to inject into humans in the form of life-saving medicine. The success of this $100 billion-dollar-plus industry relies on a standard, repeatable, testable, and safe process.

First, the process starts with Chinese hamster ovarian cells (CHO cells). CHO cells are used because of their qualities for efficient and healthy growth. Not all cells grow the same way, as quickly or as richly as these. In fact, CHO cells are the most frequently used host for the industrial production of therapeutic proteins. CHO cells are suitable for large-scale cultivation, as they grow to very high density in suspension cultures in large bioreactors They are relatively stable in the expression of heterologous genes over time. [259] Think of growing plants in your home garden—some are easier, and more predictable, to take care of, while others are finicky and require frequent attention and care.

The core of this business at this facility is manufacturing and distributing purified proteins coming from living cells. What

---

259 López-Meza, Julián, Diana Araíz-Hernández, Leydi Maribel Carrillo-Cocom, Felipe López-Pacheco, María del Refugio Rocha-Pizaña, and Mario Moisés Alvarez. 2015. "Using Simple Models To Describe The Kinetics Of Growth, Glucose Consumption, And Monoclonal Antibody Formation In Naive And Infliximab Producer CHO Cells." Cytotechnology 68 (4): 1287-1300. doi:10.1007/s10616-015-9889-

does this mean operationally? "It means keeping the cells happy," said my friend. "This means monitoring their glucose concentration, their growth process, their nutrient levels, moving and jostling the cells." Biopharmaceutical operations such as this one work 24/7, 365 days a year to keep the process safe, profitable, and to keep the cells "happy." This requires global teams of dedicated, talented people who believe the work they are doing is pushing the biopharma future frontier, and humanity, forward. Employees have to keep a close watch on every step of the cell growth and protein extraction process from start to finish. Without a completely sanitary operation working around the clock, their operation cannot succeed.

Each part of the facility is subject to FDA reviews and audits, and international audits from every country AstraZeneca ships their medicines to. While the process has been engineered extensively to reduce variability in the growth process, every once in a while, a mistake or out-of-spec finding tests the company's tolerance for error.

As we walked down the hallway, my friend pointed out a red metric that indicated a single error. "That was a $4,000 mistake." Any mistake in this facility is extremely expensive. The nutrient content, temperature, movement, and fluid levels of the cells must be kept within precise ranges at all times. A single leak or contamination could result in the loss of millions of dollars, depending on the severity of the deviation. As such, companies like AstraZeneca have gone through great lengths to develop incredible controls, efficiencies, and purity tests that have passed the FDA's most stringent regulations. The strength of these controls and efficiencies is what makes their business so reliable and, combined with great scientific prowess, profitable. Some companies, despite promising molecules in the labs, fail to meet the stringent FDA requirements and inspections and never make it to market.

THE INVESTMENT SHIFT: TRADITIONAL PHARMACEUTICAL TO BIOPHARMACEUTICALS

While rare diseases are harder to observe and treat as they happen in small subsets of populations, cancer is a disease that affects many more individuals and is, thus, a very profitable business model to focus innovative therapies around. The American Cancer Society estimates that as many as one in three individuals will develop a cancer disease during their lifetime.

Why are these medicines so groundbreaking? There's evidence that they're more effective than traditional chemically based drugs. CAR-T therapies is patient-specialized. "Much of the biotech work done at AZ is based on broad mutations found in many people with similar cancers," said Hannah. For asthma, for example, some people need only one dose of FASENRA®.

As mentioned in previous chapters, there's been an industry shift away from pills and tablets as patents expire and more research in biopharmaceuticals has shown significant outcomes. Growing cells is a science, and AstraZeneca has the capital and capacity to operate at productivity levels that small biotech companies don't have. Due to various levels of subsidized and government-negotiated healthcare prices in many countries around the world, the U.S. market ends up footing most of the bill for research and development for many biotech companies. While the final selling prices of some of these medicines is a hefty dose of sticker shock, what many don't realize is just how expensive it is for the private sector to develop and manufacture this type of technology. Only about one in one hundred molecules ever makes it to market. Not only does each molecule go through extensive efficacy studies in animals and then humans, but because of the unique nature of using living cells to manufacture proteins, each medicine requires millions of hours of science and engineering behind it to guarantee a consistent product. It can take upwards of ten years or more from the time of discovery until a treatment is viable for purchase. During this time, the company only spends money to develop that medicine. A potential medicine could fail at any point during the development process, and it's back to the drawing board. The company makes no money off of medicines during the development phase.

Traditional drugs follow a traditional demand curve where the drug is introduced, grows to maturity or peak sales (usually three to seven years after launch), starts its decline, and eventually faces generic competition or phase out. For these traditional therapies, there is an advantage to being the first to market. Normally, these traditional drugs are expected to achieve their peak sales and will deliver significant top-line revenue for the better part of two decades.[260]

---

260 "The Impact Of Gene And Cell Therapy On The Supply Chain – Clinical Trials Arena." 2018. Clinical Trials Arena.

Assuming gene and cell therapies are indeed truly curative, they will likely follow a non-traditional demand curve. In this case, it is assumed that peak sales will be achieved very quickly, compared to a traditional drug, after launch. Additionally, it is likely that once peak sales are reached, there will be a rapid decline in underlying patient demand, eventually leading to a long-term demand plateau. This assumes that once a safe and effective curative treatment is introduced, it will be able to treat the existing large pool of patents for a particular disease.[261]

AstraZeneca is one of the pharmaceutical "machines" and has ironed out the drug development process from start to finish. Only a handful of firms globally can manufacture biopharmaceuticals predictably, safely, and in such quantities. AstraZeneca's ability to predictably harvest proteins within a definite time rage, with exact temperatures and nutrient contents, hinges on their incredible ability to reduce variations to minuscule amounts between batches. The idea is to make what was previously believed to be an unpredictable process predictable and controllable.

Currently, we are unable to determine to what degree genetics and the environment are intertwined. Cells growing outside of a living organism may express proteins differently, live differently, and survive and replicate differently than those in a living organism. The industrial trick is to emulate the conditions inside an organism rather than growing cells in a Petri dish or plastic tube. "Life is complex, and not at all simple, and so is the business of growing cells," said my friend.

---

261 Ibid.

The biopharmaceutical industry is a niche wherein mathematical modeling has been widely used. Although mammalian cells have been employed for many years in the production of biotherapeutics, information related to their kinetic parameters, until recently, hasn't been widespread.[262] This facility demonstrates, however, that the two can be combined to bioengineer life in predictable, controllable ways.

One of the next steps into the biopharma cell therapy breakthrough is better emulating environments to grow and nourish cells efficiently so they are healthy and express the desired proteins in abundance, more efficiently, on a larger sale, and more cost effectively.

WHAT CELLULAR THERAPIES MIGHT MEAN

The expectation is that companies like AstraZeneca will build more of these cell manufacturing facilities to continue growing the proteins needed for innovative cancer therapies, as well as other therapies. These cellular growth facilities are being developed internationally as well, particularly in Asia. With expectations that cancer rates will remain high and even grow, and as we continue investing in our precision medicine future, we can expect that more of our drug manufacturing facilities will look like this one. What's encouraging is a recent announcement of a reduction in cancer

---

262 López-Meza, Julián, Diana Araíz-Hernández, Leydi Maribel Carrillo-Cocom, Felipe López-Pacheco, María del Refugio Rocha-Pizaña, and Mario Moisés Alvarez. 2015. "Using Simple Models To Describe The Kinetics Of Growth, Glucose Consumption, And Monoclonal Antibody Formation In Naive And Infliximab Producer CHO Cells." Cytotechnology 68 (4): 1287-1300. doi:10.1007/s10616-015-9889-

deaths worldwide, influenced by more effective, innovative new cancer therapies like CAR T cell therapies, highlighted in chapter 11. A report from The American Cancer Society has identified the largest single-year decline, 2.1 percent in the U.S. cancer death rate to date.[263] Rather than combining chemicals, they're growing and harvesting cells in the biopharma future.

263 Siegel, Rebecca L., Kimberly D. Miller, and Ahmedin Jemal. 2020. "Cancer Statistics, 2020." CA: A Cancer Journal For Clinicians 70 (1): 7-30. doi:10.3322/caac.21590.

CHAPTER 15:

PRECISION MEDICINE AND TECHNOLOGY POSE OTHER POSSIBILITIES IN HEALTHCARE

———

"There's almost 8 billion humans on the earth and 5 billion (of them) don't have access to surgery."[264]

–SCOTT HUENNEKENS, GOOGLE VERB CEO

Technology has increased the number of scans, information, and data points we can capture for each patient. The next step may be seamlessly integrating all of this information—having devices interconnect and developing new devices for new procedures, combining images, measurements, and other data points with our genome. This is one possibility with

———

264 Farr, Christina. 2018. "Why Google Co-Founder Sergey Brin Was Using A Robot To Put Sutures In Synthetic Tissue." CNBC.

5G and the Internet of Things (in healthcare known as the Internet of Medical Things). Imagine a world where you can one day video chat with your doctor rather than going for a patient visit, and they are able to review your medical activity through wearable devices integrated into your iPhone. Your bills may be less expensive, and your outcomes may be better if the devices can accurately synthesize this information and make predictions. Rather than being monitored and measured once, you could upload these data points continuously, with the device itself programmed to identify meaningful variations or irregular patterns as warning signs.

ROBOTIC SURGERY: THE FUTURE?

Medtronic, the world's largest medical device company, is one example of a firm building the future of combining data and robotics to assist surgeons. They recently acquired Mazor Robotics in 2017 for $1.7 billion to apply new possibilities with robotics to spine surgeries.[265] This acquisition may have implications for the company's other business units as well and applications to other possible surgeries one day.

Johnson and Johnson's medical device business has initiated a partnership with Google called Verb Surgical.[266] The idea with this partnership, similar to Medtronic's, is to invest in the future of robotics surgery. A robotics surgery future may result in less variation between patient procedures by controlling for differences in training, education, and skill level between surgeons. This can also increase efficiencies in the

---

265 Perriello, Brad. 2018. "Mazor Robotics Acquired By Medtronic In $1.7B Deal." The Robot Report.
266 "Our History | Verb Surgical." 2020. Verb Surgical.

number of surgeries a surgeon can perform. A variety of imaging and testing equipment can assist surgeons in planning a procedure and provide more information and visibility before and during a patient procedure. Manual surgery is limited to the doctor's small hand tools, eyes, experience, fatigue, and judgment.

New capabilities like stem cell implants mean the need for all kinds of new instruments and tools for new procedures. With these new capabilities, we'll see the rise, and are already seeing the rise, of new tools, instruments, and devices to deliver these new possibilities.

This may sound like a moonshot for healthcare's future, but it may increase efficiencies and reduce wait times per procedure and improve patient outcomes. It may also allow us to learn at an accelerated pace as we continue to pave the way forward for our precision medicine future. This may ultimately translate to more cost-effective error-free surgeries with fewer wait times, and an enhanced capacity to perform more surgery.

Think about the improvements we've made across other industries as a result of automation, better tools, and seamless data integration. Car production times have been dramatically reduced: first with the development of Henry Ford's assembly line, then with the gradual replacement of human labor by machines. We're able to make better cars with less time and effort, at affordable prices globally. We can spend more time planning the design of the car than on its physical production.

Imagine a world as well where robots are used to perform more minimally invasive surgeries. The surgeon is the operator of the machine, controlling it from a console. The surgeon's view of the procedure isn't limited by the acuity of their own eyes but enhanced by cameras and magnification power provided by the machine. The surgeon is less likely to become fatigued during the procedure with the help of robotic tools. With more data, cameras, and constant streams of information from many angles, automated surgeries may be less prone to error and could result in better patient outcomes. This will, of course, require a cultural shift in thinking on the part of physicians and healthcare professionals. It will also require a shift in thinking in the patient's mind. Some of this future thinking is already becoming a reality.

In the 2000s, the da Vinci, an autonomous robotic surgical machine, was unveiled, priced around $2 million per machine. The idea was it could, among other things, reduce variation between surgery times and procedures, and with a continuous amount of data, allow machines to "learn." It can also reduce the amount of planning time that goes into each patient surgery.[267] The da Vinci is, however, only the beginning.

FUTURE STATE

The end state for this may one day be that physicians train with the robotic surgical machines with virtual reality. They could one day mean performing surgical procedures remotely, on the other side of the world, even. This may be

---

267 2020. Davincisurgery.com.

one potential outcome of an integrated medical technology system, and one that may be coming sooner than we think. Are we ready to accept the help of robotics tools such as these in delivering our healthcare?

SEEING THE BIOPHARMA FUTURE CONCLUSION

—

"We've arranged a civilization in which most crucial elements profoundly depend on science and technology."

−CARL SAGAN[268]

When I was twenty-five and just back from Peace Corps service, I realized technology had changed the world. I was unsure of what jobs I could perform with low vision. I was grappling with trying to understand what I'd ignored for years and whether I really did have Stargardt's disease. I doubted my own abilities; some physicians did too. However, when I realized that technological advancement had also changed possibilities in healthcare, my mindset shifted.

As soon as I read about stem cell therapies being applied to patients with Stargardt's disease, I immediately set up

---

268 "Carl Sagan." 2020. Biography.

appointments with some of the best eye hospitals in the country at places like the Johns Hopkins Wilmer Eye Institute. It took more than one year to get an appointment at Johns Hopkins. Many days, I was discouraged and wondered if treatment would ever happen, but I never lost hope. Five years later, one doctor's research is beginning to bear fruit and may result in the rise of entirely new instruments to deliver stem cells to replenish those that have been damaged by Stargardt's and other diseases—the future looks bright.

In the course of writing this, seeing Francois pass away from cancer, launching a career in pharmaceuticals, finishing my MBA at Georgetown, and making slow progress on my own journey toward treatment, I've learned to never give up. Progress is slow, but it *is* possible and is happening across the medical and healthcare communities. What's most inspiring to me is that the progress and the conversations are truly global. And in the course of writing this, I wrote my way to a new chapter in life and a new career in the pharmaceuticals industry in Princeton, NJ. I'm working and writing for industries and companies I believe are changing the world for the better and improving healthcare.

WHY INVEST IN PRECISION MEDICINE?

Innovation in science enabled us to domesticate animals, develop modern agriculture, develop modern medicine, and has improved the quality of our lives. We must keep innovating; we must imagine, believe, and invest in the future to survive and progress as a society.

The inspiring doctors I met were right—we've made tremendous progress in the last fifteen years in genomics and precision medicine. The hope is that we can continue developing more effective treatments for diseases, as well as preventing and treating them earlier. Some of this progress is due to a culmination of scientific discoveries and timing. The progress we've made has been possible because of investments like yours. Proceeds from *Seeing the Biopharma Future* are donated to gene therapy and stem cell research and the development of new tools and technologies at Johns Hopkins. This helps treat rare genetic eye diseases like my own, and multitudes of others.

Some doctors were and still are pessimistic about potential treatments—how much can we learn from the genome, CRISPR gene editing, gene therapies, and CAR T-cell therapies to treat diseases, they ask. It's true that we understand very little of the genome and how it works. It's true that our ability to apply it to clinical treatment and develop new medicines is limited. It's true that genetics doesn't decide everything. It's also true that we've made tremendous progress and a number of scientific breakthroughs like the three outlined in this book emerged at a time when the world is more connected than ever. Now, more is possible; there has been a global recognition that investing in initiatives such as these can improve human health and will shape our future as a species.

These breakthroughs have renewed my hope and confidence in the future of innovative medicine and its possibilities. This has improved my performance at work and my belief that I can adapt to new challenges. Even if we don't develop a cure for Stargardt's in my lifetime, I have to invest in the precision medicine future not only for myself but for humanity. What better purpose to devote your life to than developing new, innovative treatments to improving the lives of others? It's also why I'm asking you to share what you've learned about the future of genomics and precision medicine with your friends, family, and colleagues.

JOINING THE PRECISION MEDICINE CONVERSATION

By making this investment, you're joining a community and a conversation of individuals who believe in innovation and recognize the need to improve our healthcare system in the twenty-first century. As curious science enthusiasts, you're investing in cutting edge research at one of the world's best hospitals—Johns Hopkins. As business professionals, you're investing in the work of companies like Illumina and Bristol Myers Squibb, who are applying genomics information to developing more effective drugs for patients. As patients, you're investing in developing treatments for a whole host of diseases. Learn more at clinicaltrials.gov, and ask your doctor to refer you to an ongoing study that may impact you. If you have your genome sequenced, it helps us all progress in learning more about the genome and its applications to health and our future as a species. See how you can get involved in Google's Project Baseline to develop new medical devices and insights into human health. It's individuals like you that can see this biopharma future and invest in it to make it a reality.

If you'd like to join other conversations on the ethical use of genomics data, or contact me, you can find me at LinkedIn: https://www.linkedin.com/in/abra-sitler-34b56387/.

"Imagination will often carry us to worlds that never were, or could be. But without it, we go nowhere."

—CARL SAGAN

APPENDIX

INTRODUCTION

Danchin, Antoine. The Delphic Boat. Harvard University Press. 2002.

Devitt, Michael. 2020. "CDC Data Show U.S. Life Expectancy Continues to Decline." Aafp.org. https://www.aafp.org/news/health-of-the-public/20181210lifeexpectdrop.html

International Consortium Completes Human Genome Project." 2020. Genome.gov. https://www.genome.gov/11006929/2003-release-international-consortium-completes-hgp

"The Cost of Sequencing a Human Genome." 2020. Genome.gov. https://directorsblog.nih.gov/2018/02/06/sequencing-human-genome-with-pocket-sized-nanopore-device/

2020. Who.Int. https://www.who.int/healthinfo/paper30.pdf.

CHAPTER 1

Reference, Genetics. 2020. "What Is Precision Medicine?" Genetics Home Reference https://ghr.nlm.nih.gov/primer/precision-medicine/initiative

"BRCA Mutations: Cancer Risk and Genetic Testing Fact Sheet." 2020. National Cancer Institute. https://ghr.nlm.nih.gov/primer/precisionmedicine/definition

"NIH Research Portfolio Online Reporting Tools (Report)." 2020. Report.Nih.gov. https://report.nih.gov/NIHfactsheets/ViewFactSheet.aspx?csid=45.

Verma, AshishSwarup, Shruti Rastogi, Shishir Agrahari, and Anchal Singh. 2011. "Biotechnology in the Realm of History." Journal of Pharmacy and Bioallied Sciences 3 (3): 321. doi:10.4103/0975-7406.84430.

David O'Riordan. Engineers Ireland. 2013. "Transitioning From Traditional Pharmaceuticals to Biopharma – Engineers Journal." Engineers Journal. http://www.engineersjournal.ie/2013/10/17/transitioning-from-traditional-pharmaceuticals-to-biopharma/.

"Stargardt's Disease | National Eye Institute." 2020. Nei.Nih.gov. https://www.nei.nih.gov/learn-about-eye-health/eye-conditions-and-diseases/stargardt-disease.

"Vitamin A." 2020. Mayo Clinic. https://www.mayoclinic.org/drugs-supplements-vitamin-a/art-20365945.

"Stargardt's Disease Vitamin A Contraindication – Natural Eye Care Blog: News & Research on Vision." 2012. Natural Eye Care Blog: News & Research on Vision. https://www.naturaleyecare. com/blog/stargardts-disease-vitamin-a-contraindication/.\

"An Eye to A Cure." 2011. NIH Intramural Research Program. https://irp.nih.gov/our-research/research-in-action/an-eye-to-a-cure.

Lipofuscin: MedlinePlus Medical Encyclopedia." 2020. Medline-plus.gov. https://medlineplus.gov/ency/article/00224

"Stargardt's Disease | National Eye Institute." 2020. Nei.Nih.gov. https://www.nei.nih.gov/learn-about-eye-health/eye-condi-tions-and-diseases/stargardt-disease.

"Mendel's Laws: Law of Independent Assortment, Segregation, Dominance, Inheritance." 2017. Science ABC. https://www. scienceabc.com/humans/gregor-mendels-laws-of-inheri-tance-law-of-segregation-dominance-independent-assortment. html.

"Keeping Up With Stem Cell Therapies. – Rising Tide Biology." 2020. Rising Tide Biology. https://www.risingtidebio.com/ history-stem-cell-therapy-benefits/

"DNA Sequencing Costs: Data." 2020. Genome.gov. https://www. genome.gov/about-genomics/fact-sheets/DNA-Sequencing-Costs-Data.

CHAPTER 2

Automating Medical Records in the 21St Century." 2020. Health-careadministration.com. http://www.healthcareadministra-tion.com/automating-medical-records-in-the-21st-century/.

"The Medical Record (R)Evolution." 2020. Forbes.com. https://www.forbes.com/sites/carolynmcclanahan/2012/02/21/the-medi-cal-record-revolution/#a36673549330.

Evans, R. S. 2016. "Electronic Health Records: Then, Now, and in the Future." Yearbook of Medical Informatics 25 (S 01): S48-S61. doi:10.15265/iys-2016-s006.

Fontenot, Sarah. 2020. "The Affordable Care Act and Electronic Health Records. 2013. Sarahfontenot.com. https://sarahfonte-not.com/wp-content/uploads/2015/04/5-Dec-2013-Will-EHRs-Improve-Quality-Article.pdf.

CHAPTER 3

"CAR T-Cell Therapy: How Payers Are Responding to Huge Price Tags." 2020. Managed Healthcare Executive. https://www.managedhealthcareexecutive.com/non-hodgkin-lymphoma/car-t-cell-therapy-how-payers-are-responding-huge-price-tags.

(US), National, Institute (US), Steven Woolf, and Laudan Aron. 2013. "Public Health and Medical Care Systems." National Academies Press (US). https://www.ncbi.nlm.nih.gov/books/NBK154484/.

Deloitte Health Outlook. 2020. Www2.Deloitte.com. https://www2.
deloitte.com/content/dam/Deloitte/global/Documents/Life-
Sciences-Health-Care/gx-lshc-2016-health-care-outlook.pdf.

2020. Who.Int. https://www.who.int/healthinfo/paper30.pd

"U.S. Health Care Costs Rise Faster Than Inflation." 2020. Forbes.
com. https://www.forbes.com/sites/mikepatton/2015/06/29/u-
s-health-care-costs-rise-faster-than-inflation/#7d48ad996fa1.

"New Study Explains Why US Health Care Spending Increased
$1 Trillion." 2017. Institute for Health Metrics and Evaluation.
http://www.healthdata.org/news-release/new-study-explains-
why-us-health-care-spending-increased-1-trillion.

"New Survey Reveals 57 % of Americans Have Been Surprised by a
Medical Bill | NORC.org." 2020. Norc.org. https://www.norc.
org/NewsEventsPublications/PressReleases/Pages/new-sur-
vey-reveals-57-%-of-americans-have-been-surprised-by-a-
medical-bill.aspx.

Sussman, Anna. 2020. "Burden of Health-Care Costs Moves to
The Middle Class." WSJ.

Emanuel, Ezekiel. 2019. "Big Pharma's Go-To Defense of Soaring
Drug Prices Doesn't Add Up." The Atlantic.

Behind Your Rising Health-Care Bills: Secret Hospital Deals That
Squelch Competition – WellNet Healthcare." 2018. WellNet
Healthcare. https://WellNet.com/broker-resource/news/
behind-rising-health-

"Why Do Healthcare Costs Keep Rising?" 2020. Investopedia. https://www.investopedia.com/insurance/why-do-healthcare-costs-keep-rising/.

Sussman, Anna. 2020. "Burden of Health-Care Costs Moves to The Middle Class." WSJ. https://www.wsj.com/articles/burden-of-health-care-costs-moves-to-the-middle-class-1472166246

Kliff, Sarah. 2013. One hospital charges $8,000 — another, $38,000. Washington Post. https://www.washingtonpost.com/news/wonk/wp/2013/05/08/one-hospital-charges-8000-another-38000/

Behind Your Rising Health-Care Bills: Secret Hospital Deals That Squelch Competition – WellNet Healthcare." 2018. WellNet Healthcare. https://WellNet.com/broker-resource/news/behind-rising-health-care-bills/.

"Building A System That Works: The Future of Health Care | Health Affairs." 2020. Healthaffairs.org. https://www.healthaffairs.org/do/10.1377/hb

"What's Keeping Us So Busy in Primary Care? A Snapshot From One Practice | NEJM." 2020. New England Journal of Medicine. https://www.nejm.org/doi/full/10.1056/NEJMon0910793.

"Key Facts About the Uninsured Population." 2019. The Henry J. Kaiser Family Foundation. https://www.kff.org/uninsured/issue-brief/key-facts-about-the-uninsured-population/.

CHAPTER 4

Park, Alice. 2014. "Stem Cells Allow Nearly Blind Patient to See."
Time. https://time.com/3507094/stem-cells-eyesight/

"Report Shows US Brand-Name Drug Prices 'Highest in The
World'." 2019. European Pharmaceutical Review. https://www.
europeanpharmaceuticalreview.com/news/87383/us-drug-
prices-highest-world/.

DiMasi, Joseph A, Ronald W Hansen, and Henry G Grabowski.
2003. "The Price of Innovation: New Estimates of Drug Development Costs." Journal of Health Economics 22 (2): 151-185.
doi:10.1016/s0167-6296(02)00126-1.

"Topic: Pharmaceutical Industry in The U.S.." 2020. Www.Statista.
com. https://www.statista.com/topics/1719/pharmaceutical-in-
dustry/.

"Age-Related Macular Degeneration (AMD) Data and Statistics |
National Eye Institute." 2020. Nei.Nih.gov. https://www.nei.
nih.gov/learn-about-eye-health/resources-for-health-educa-
tors/eye-health-data-and-statistics/age-related-macular-de-
generation-amd-data-and-statistics.

"What Is Hatch-Waxman?" 2020. Phrma.org. https://www.phrma.
org/fact-sheet/what-is-hatch-waxman.

THOMAS MORROW, Linda Hull Felcone. 2004. "Defining the
Difference: What Makes Biologics Unique." Biotechnology
Healthcare 1 (4): 24. https://www.ncbi.nlm.nih.gov/pmc/arti-
cles/

CHAPTER 5

"Francis Crick." 2020. Profiles in Science. https://profiles.nlm.nih. gov/spotlight/sc.

Reference, Genetics. 2020. "What Is DNA?" Genetics Home Reference. https://ghr.nlm.nih.gov/primer/basics/dn

Lessons from the Human Genome Project. 2018. https://www.youtube.com/watch?v=qOW5e4BgEa4

DNA Sequencing Costs: Data." 2020. Genome.gov. https://www.genome.gov/about-genomics/fact-sheets/DNA-Sequencing-Costs-Data.

Dr. Leming Shi, National Center for Toxicological Research. "MicroArray Quality Control (MAQC) Project". U.S. Food and Drug Administration. Retrieved 2007-12-26.

Goetz, Thomas 2017 "23AndMe Will Decode Your DNA for $1,000. Welcome to the Age of Genomics".

CHAPTER 6

"Focus: New Machines Can Sequence Human Genome in One Hour, Illumina Announces." 2017. San Diego Union-Tribune. https://www.sandiegouniontribune.com/business/biotech/sd-me-illumina-novaseq-20170109-story.html.

"Difference Between DNA Genotyping & Sequencing." 2020. 23Andme Customer Care. https://customercare.23andme.com/hc/en-us/articles/202904600-Difference-Between-DNA-Genotyping-Sequencing.

"Microarray Analysis Techniques." 2020. En.Wikipedia.org. https://en.wikipedia.org/wiki/Microarray_analysis_techniques.

"Nucleic Acid Hybridization." 2015. En.Wikipedia.org. https://en.wikipedia.org/wiki/Nucleic_acid_hybridization.

"Fluorescent Tag." 2020. En.Wikipedia.org. https://en.wikipedia.org/wiki/Fluorescent_tag.

Swarns, Rachel. 2017. "With DNA Testing, Adoptees Find A Way to Connect With Family." Nytimes.com. https://www.nytimes.com/2012/01/24/us/with-dna-testing-adoptees-find-a-way-to-connect-with-family.html?pagewanted=all&_r=0.

23Andme." 2020. En.Wikipedia.org. https://en.wikipedia.org/wiki/23andMe#cite_note-Jeffries-28.

"Mitochondrial DNA." 2020. En.Wikipedia.org. https://en.wikipedia.org/wiki/Mitochondrial_DNA.

"Gene." 2020. En.Wikipedia.org. https://en.wikipedia.org/wiki/Gene.

"Genealogical DNA Test." 2020. En.Wikipedia.org. https://en.wikipedia.org/wiki/Genealogical_DNA_test.

"Haplogroup." 2020. En.Wikipedia.org. https://en.wikipedia.org/wiki/Haplogroup.

"Difference Between DNA Genotyping & Sequencing." 2020. 23Andme Customer Care. https://customercare.23andme.

com/hc/en-us/articles/202904600-Difference-Between-DNA-Genotyping-Sequencing.

"Alpha-1 Antitrypsin Deficiency." 2020. En.Wikipedia.org. https://en.wikipedia.org/wiki/Alpha-1_antitrypsin_deficiency.

"Glucose-6-Phosphate Dehydrogenase Deficiency." 2020. En.Wikipedia.org. https://en.wikipedia.org/wiki/Glucose-6-phosphate_dehydrogenase_deficiency.

"Dystonia." 2020. En.Wikipedia.org. https://en.wikipedia.org/wiki/Dystonia.

"Haemophilia C." 2020. En.Wikipedia.org. https://en.wikipedia.org/wiki/Haemophilia_C.

"Gaucher's Disease." 2020. En.Wikipedia.org. https://en.wikipedia.org/wiki/Gaucher %27s_disease.

Editors, ZS. 2020. "DNA-Based Data Is A Hot Commodity, And Pharma Is Buying." Info.Zs.com. https://info.zs.com/activeingredient/dna-based-data-is-a-hot-commodity-and-pharmas-buying.

"Using Crowd-Sourced Data to Find Genetic Links to Depression | Pfizer." 2020. Pfizer.com. https://www.pfizer.com/news/featured_stories/featured_stories_detail/using_crowd_sourced_data_to_find_genetic_links_to_depression.

CHAPTER 7

"Synthego | Full Stack Genome Engineering." 2020. Synthego.com. https://www.synthego.com/learn/genome-engineering-history.

"Hepatitis B." 2019. Who.Int. https://www.who.int/news-room/fact-sheets/detail/hepatitis-b.

"Biotech Foods Endorsed by U.N. Agency." 2004. Msnbc.com. http://www.nbcnews.com/id/4997835/ns/us_news-environ-ment/t/biotech-foods-endorsed-un-agency/#.XGNSBDM3lPY.

Shinya Yamanaka, PhD. 2020. "Shinya Yamanaka | UCSF Pro-files." Profiles.Ucsf.Edu. https://profiles.ucsf.edu/shinya.yamanaka.

S, Takahashi. 2020. "Induction of Pluripotent Stem Cells From Mouse Embryonic and Adult Fibroblast Cultures by Defined Factors. – PubMed – NCBI." Ncbi.Nlm.Nih.gov. https://www.ncbi.nlm.nih.gov/pubmed/16904174.

"Questions and Answers About CRISPR." 2014. Broad Institute. https://www.broadinstitute.org/what-broad/areas-focus/proj-ect-spotlight/questions-and-answers-about-crispr.

Zhang, Feng. 2015. "CRISPR/Cas9: Prospects and Chal-lenges." Human Gene Therapy 26 (7): 409-410. doi:10.1089/hum.2015.29002.fzh.

Nagaich, Upendra. 2015. "Recombinant DNA Technology: A Revolutionizing Outlook." Journal of Advanced Pharma-ceutical Technology and Research 6 (4): 147. doi:10.4103/2231-4040.166456.

Ledford, Heidi. 2015. "Salmon Approval Heralds Rethink of Transgenic Animals." Nature 527 (7579): 417-418. doi:10.1038/527417a.

"Overfishing." 2020. World Wildlife Fund. https://www.worldwildlife.org/threats/overfishing.

"Synthego | Full Stack Genome Engineering." 2020. Synthego.com. https://www.synthego.com/learn/genome-engineering-history.

Doudna, Jennifer. 2020. "How CRISPR Lets Us Edit Our DNA." Ted.com. https://www.ted.com/talks/jennifer_doudna_how_crispr_lets_us_edit_our_dna/up-next.

CHAPTER 8

"MD Anderson Immunologist Jim Allison Awarded Nobel Prize." 2020. MD Anderson Cancer Center. https://www.mdanderson.org/newsroom/md-anderson-immunologist-jim-allison-awarded-nobel-prize.h00-159228090.html.

Lino, Christopher A., Jason C. Harper, James P. Carney, and Jerilyn A. Timlin. 2018. "Delivering CRISPR: A Review of The Challenges and Approaches." Drug Delivery 25 (1): 1234-1257. doi:10.1080/10717544.2018.1474964.

Zhang, Feng. 2015. "CRISPR/Cas9: Prospects and Challenges." Human Gene Therapy 26 (7): 409-410. doi:10.1089/hum.2015.29002.fzh.

"US Companies Launch CRISPR Clinical Trial." 2020. The Scientist Magazine®. https://www.the-scientist.com/news-opinion/us-companies-launch-crispr-clinical-trial-64746.

"A Safety and Efficacy Study Evaluating CTX001 In Subjects With Transfusion-Dependent B-Thalassemia – Full Text View – Clinicaltrials.gov." 2020. Clinicaltrials.gov. https://clinicaltrials.gov/ct2/show/NCT03655678.

"Genes and Human Diseases." 2020. World Health Organization. https://www.who.int/genomics/public/geneticdiseases/en/index2.html.

"Pipeline – Intellia Therapeutics." 2020. Intellia Therapeutics. https://www.intelliatx.com/pipeline-2/.

"Editas Medicine." 2020. Editas Medicine. https://www.editasmedicine.com/.

Regalado, Antonio. 2020. "EXCLUSIVE: Chinese Scientists Are Creating CRISPR Babies." MIT Technology Review. https://www.technologyreview.com/s/612458/exclusive-chinese-scientists-are-creating-crispr-babies/.

Banks, Marcus, Greg Uyeno, Amy Nordrum, Jeanette Ferrara, Peter Hess, and Marcus Banks. 2018. "First CRISPR Clinical Trial Begins in Europe | Scienceline." Scienceline. https://scienceline.org/2018/11/first-crispr-clinical-trial-begins-in-europe/.

"Questions and Answers About CRISPR." 2014. Broad Institute. https://www.broadinstitute.org/what-broad/areas-focus/project-spotlight/questions-and-answers-about-crispr.

"NIST Genome Editing Consortium." 2020. NIST. https://www.nist.gov/programs-projects/nist-genome-editing-consortium.

GATLIN, ALLISON. 2018. "CRISPR Gene Editing And 3 Biotech Companies Blaze New Path to Cures | Stock News & Stock Market Analysis – IBD." Investor's Business Daily. https://www.investors.com/news/technology/crispr-gene-editing-biotech-companies/.

CHAPTER 9

Danchin, Antoine. 2009. "Bacteria as Computers Making Computers." FEMS Microbiology Reviews 33 (1): 3-26. doi:10.1111/j.1574-6976.2008.00137.x.

"Artificial Intelligence." 2020. En.Wikipedia.org. https://en.wikipedia.org/wiki/Artificial_intelligence.

"Molecular Genetics." 2012. En.Wikipedia.org. https://en.wikipedia.org/wiki/Molecular_genetics.

"Model of Computation." 2020. En.Wikipedia.org. https://en.wikipedia.org/wiki/Model_of_computation.

Inc., Global. 2020. "Precision Medicine Market Size to Exceed $87 Billion By 2023: Global Market Insights Inc." Prnewswire.com. https://www.prnewswire.com/news-releases/precision-medicine-market-size-to-exceed-87-billion-by-2023-global-market-insights-inc-599454691.html.

"IBM Watson For Genomics – Overview – United States." 2020. Ibm.com. https://www.ibm.com/us-en/marketplace/watson-for-genomics.

"Xconomy: Alphabet's Biotech R&D Arm Verily Raises $1B To Fuel Growth." 2019. Xconomy. https://xconomy.com/san-francisco/2019/01/03/alphabets-biotech-rd-arm-verily-raises-1b-to-fuel-growth/.

"Microsoft Genomics." 2020. Microsoft Genomics. https://www.microsoft.com/en-us/genomics/.

"YouTube." 2020. YouTube.com. https://www.youtube.com/watch?v=HsfojplqbMI.

"Healthcare and Life Sciences On AWS." 2020. Amazon Web Services, Inc. https://aws.amazon.com/health/.

"1000 Genomes Project And AWS." 2020. Amazon Web Services, Inc. https://aws.amazon.com/1000genomes/.

Regalado, Antonio. 2020. "Exclusive: Apple Pursues DNA Data." MIT Technology Review. https://www.technologyreview.com/s/537081/apple-has-plans-for-your-dna/.

WIRE, BUSINESS. 2018. "National Institutes of Health Awards Palantir With Contract to Advance Critical Health Research." Businesswire.com. https://www.businesswire.com/news/home/20180921005056/en/National-Institutes-Health-Awards %C2 %A0Palantir-Contract-Advance %C2 %A0Critical %C2 %A0Health %C2 %A0Research.

GeneBank, China. 2020. "China National GeneBank." Cngb.org. https://www.cngb.org/index.html?i18nlang=en_US.

Flynn, Megan. 2019. "A Harvard scientist is developing a DNA-based dating app." The Washington Post. https://www.washingtonpost.com/nation/2019/12/13/genetics-george-church-dna-dating-app-reduce-disease-eugenics/

"Human Genome Project FAQ." 2020. Genome.gov. https://www.genome.gov/human-genome-project/Completion-FAQ.

"Asimov — Intelligent Design." 2020. Asimov.Io. https://www.asimov.io/.

Wiggers, Kyle. 2019. "Alphabet's Verily Raises $1 Billion To Make Health Care Smarter." VentureBeat. https://venturebeat.com/2019/01/03/alphabets-verily-raises-1-billion-to-make-health-care-smarter/.

Olanubi, Sijuola. 2016. "Top Five Largest Cloud Companies in The World – Tharawat Magazine." Tharawat Magazine. https://www.tharawat-magazine.com/facts/top-5-largest-cloud-companies-world/#gs.s2xchp.

CHAPTER 10

"Cancer Statistics." 2018. National Cancer Institute. https://www.cancer.gov/about-cancer/understanding/statistics.

CHAPTER 11

Arruebo, Manuel, Nuria Vilaboa, Berta Sáez-Gutierrez, Julio Lambea, Alejandro Tres, Mónica Valladares, and África González-Fernández. 2011. "Assessment of The Evolution of Cancer Treatment Therapies." Cancers 3 (3): 3279-3330. doi:10.3390/cancers3033279.

"MD Anderson Immunologist Jim Allison Awarded Nobel Prize." 2020. MD Anderson Cancer Center. https://www.mdanderson.org/newsroom/md-anderson-immunologist-jim-allison-awarded-nobel-prize.h00-159228090.html.

"The Nobel Prize in Physiology or Medicine 2018." 2020. Nobelprize.org. https://www.nobelprize.org/prizes/medicine/2018/allison/facts/.

"FDA Approval Brings First Gene Therapy to The United States." 2018. U.S. Food and Drug Administration. https://www.fda.gov/news-events/press-announcements/fda-approval-brings-first-gene-therapy-united-states.

FADEN, RUTH R., KALIPSO CHALKIDOU, JOHN APPLEBY, HUGH R. WATERS, and JONATHON P. LEIDER. 2009. "Expensive Cancer Drugs: A Comparison Between the United States and the United Kingdom." Milbank Quarterly 87 (4): 789-819. doi:10.1111/j.1468-0009.2009.00579.x.

CHAPTER 12

"What's Behind the Pharmaceutical Sector's M&A Push." 2020. McKinsey & Company. https://www.mckinsey.com/business-functions/strategy-and-corporate-finance/our-insights/whats-behind-the-pharmaceutical-sectors-m-and-a-push.

"Georgetown Physician Leads National Melanoma Study." 2015. Medstar Georgetown University Hospital. https://

www.medstargeorgetown.org/2015/08/03/georgetown-physi-
cian-leads-national-melanoma-study/#q={}.

Dagogo-Jack, Ibiayi, and Alice T. Shaw. 2017. "Tumour Heterogeneity and Resistance to Cancer Therapies." Nature Reviews
Clinical Oncology 15 (2): 81-94. doi:10.1038/nrclinonc.2017.166.

"Apoptosis: A Target for Anticancer Therapy." 2018. International Journal of Molecular Sciences 19 (2): 448. doi:10.3390/
ijms19020448.

CHAPTER 13

"Can China Become a Scientific Superpower?" 2019. The Economist. https://www.economist.com/science-and-technol-
ogy/2019/01/12/can-china-become-a-scientific-superpower.

"The Pursuit of Healthy China 2020 | Asia Outlook Magazine."
2020. Asia Outlook Magazine. https://www.asiaoutlookmag.
com/news/the-pursuit-of-healthy-china-2020.

"BGI Group Official Website." 2020. En.Genomics.Cn. https://
en.genomics.cn/.

"Top 10 Asia Biopharma Clusters 2018." 2018. GEN – Genetic Engineering and Biotechnology News. https://www.genengnews.
com/a-lists/top-10-asia-biopharma-clusters-2018/.

Markets, Research. 2020. "Global Strategic Evaluation of Precision
Medicine Markets 2016-2026 & Country Analysis for Emerging Opportunities."

"BGI Is A Global Genomics Organization – We Provide Fast, Accurate, Affordable Genomic Data for All Your Sequencing Needs." 2020. BGI – Global. https://www.bgi.com/us/.

"The Pursuit of Healthy China 2020 | Asia Outlook Magazine." 2020. Asia Outlook Magazine. https://www.asiaoutlookmag. com/news/the-pursuit-of-healthy-china-2020.

"Regions-BGI Group Official Website." 2020. En.Genomics.Cn. https://en.genomics.cn/en-global.html.

"China National GeneBank-BGI Group Official Website." 2020. En. Genomics.Cn. https://en.genomics.cn/en-gene.html.

"To Feed Its 1.4 Billion, China Bets Big on Genome Editing of Crops." 2019. Science | AAAS. https://www.sciencemag.org/news/2019/07/ feed-its-14-billion-china-bets-big-genome-editing-crops.

Klitzman, Robert. 2012. Am I My Genes?

"GDRD: Genetic Disease and Rare Disease Database – Cngbdb." 2020. Db.Cngb.org. https://db.cngb.org/gdrd/searchResult/ gene %20GJB2.

"OMIM – Online Mendelian Inheritance in Man." 2020. Omim. org. https://omim.org/graph/linear/304400.

2020. Asiatimes.com. https://www.asiatimes.com/2019/02/article/ chinas-genebank-boasts-20-million-samples/.

Antoine Danchin (0000-0002-6350-5001)." 2020. Orcid.org. https:// orcid.org/0000-0002-6350-5001.

"Can China Become a Scientific Superpower?" 2019. The Economist. https://www.economist.com/science-and-technology/2019/01/12/can-china-

2020. Home.Treasury.gov. https://home.treasury.gov/system/files/206/Fact-Sheet-FIRRMA-Pilot-Program.pdf?_ga=2.267558030.1031051785.1556282398-1301615180.1553899914.

CHAPTER 14

"AstraZeneca – Research-Based Biopharmaceutical Company." 2020. Astrazeneca.com. https://www.astrazeneca.com/.

López-Meza, Julián, Diana Araíz-Hernández, Leydi Maribel Carrillo-Cocom, Felipe López-Pacheco, María del Refugio Rocha-Pizaña, and Mario Moisés Alvarez. 2015. "Using Simple Models to Describe the Kinetics of Growth, Glucose Consumption, And Monoclonal Antibody Formation in Naive and Infliximab Producer CHO Cells." Cytotechnology 68 (4): 1287-1300. doi:10.1007/s10616-015-9889-2.

CHAPTER 15

Perriello, Brad. 2018. "Mazor Robotics Acquired by Medtronic in $1.7B Deal." The Robot Report. https://www.therobotreport.com/medtronic-17b-mazor-robotics/.

"Our History | Verb Surgical." 2020. Verb Surgical. https://www.verbsurgical.com/about/our-history/.

2020. Davincisurgery.com. https://www.davincisurgery.com/.

Made in the USA
Columbia, SC
25 March 2020

89949101R00152